The
Wild & Healthy
Cookbook

Nourishing Meals Inspired by Nature's Bounty

Michelle Faust Lang Berthels

Translated by Kim Gardner

Skyhorse Publishing

Contents

Skyhorse Publishing books may be purchased in bulk at special discounts
for sales promotion, corporate gifts, fund-raising, or educational purposes.
Special editions can also be created to specifications. For details, contact the
Special Sales Department, Skyhorse Publishing, 307 West 36th Street, 11th
Floor, New York, NY 10018 or info@skyhorsepublishing.com.

Skyhorse® and Skyhorse Publishing® are registered trademarks of Skyhorse
Publishing, Inc.®, a Delaware corporation.

Visit our website at www.skyhorsepublishing.com.

10 9 8 7 6 5 4 3 2 1

Library of Congress Cataloging-in-Publication Data is available on file.

Print ISBN: 978-1-5107-7880-1
Ebook ISBN: 978-1-5107-7881-8

Printed in China

Disclaimer

The herb guide in this book should be seen first and foremost as an introduction
to various plants and herbs, and is neither a handbook for self-treatment, nor
should it replace a healthy and varied diet. The information about plants and herbs
provided in this book is also not exhaustive, so use of this book's plants and herbs
is at your own risk. The author cannot be held responsible for the effects of plants
and herbs or any side effects. As neither the author nor the publisher is aware of any
allergies, sensitivities, or other reactions, your health and well-being are your sole
responsibility. Always remember to seek and consult your doctor if you are pregnant,
breastfeeding, ill, taking medication, or generally in doubt.

Introduction

Welcome to *The Wild & Healthy Cookbook* and the woman behind it

Four ingredients that form the base of the meals I create in this book are nourishment (for both mind and heart), enjoyment (without a guilty conscience), presence (in the dining experience and in my own company), and curiosity (for nature's wild raw materials).

I believe that with a good conscience, joy of food and good flavor follow. I highly value sustainability, clean and natural raw materials, leftover and surplus food, recycling, and ecology. There are only a few raw materials that I neatly avoid, but in return, I make high demands on those things I do fill my body with.

My edible kitchen garden is filled with everything from sun-ripened strawberries to flavorful herbs. My free time is spent conjuring this treasure trove into dishes that end up on the dinner table in both familiar and new compositions.

My journey toward a greener plate, however, has certainly been a long time coming, and many years passed before my vegetable adventure really took off and I discovered the hidden treasures of the plant universe. But, before I knew it, I'd replaced brown pork chops, roast beef, and pink chicken legs with crispy chickpeas, tofu chunks, and grilled vegetable skewers. So, although it took me a long time to find my inner Earth connection and enthusiasm for plants, herbs and, spices, I believe that it is never too late to explore nature's bounty.

This cookbook celebrates just a small selection of all the many magical,

interesting, and edible plants found here on Mother Earth, and invites you to be curious about what a sprinkling of herbs can do for a dish, and not least your well-being. Some of the recipes invite slowness and extra coziness, while other recipes create space for a little well-deserved break in everyday life.

I hope you will take this book with you into the kitchen and not be afraid to use it, and add your own doodles and notes when you make new discoveries or have appetizing "aha" experiences. I'll take you by the hand and show you the way.

Welcome and enjoy.

My holistic food philosophy and lifestyle

After many years of energy-sapping diets and guidelines, I have finally learned to listen to my desire and intuition, rather than tending to dietary philosophies. My body has gone through big changes since I trained as a health mentor, where I was introduced to a magical world with great treatment options, and, not least, got a holistic view of the body as a whole. I experienced a newfound love for the soft and unimaginably strong house that carries me around every day to this and that, and that love grew as I learned more about taking care of both mind and heart.

I am, therefore, neither vegan, nor vegetarian, nor pescatarian, but primarily eat a plant-based diet. I like to enjoy a piece of freshly caught fish, a soft slice of cheese every now and then, or even a bite of a grilled sausage. For me, it's about balancing my meals and making an active choice in everyday life—without worrying about the day after.

Based on the idea that my lifestyle changes every single day, I have gained greater emotional freedom by focusing on enjoyment and nourishment in my meals, rather than calories, plate composition, and demands that condemn my actions. New foods are introduced, others are released again, and if it changes in a week, it's perfectly fine, because there is no final result in my world anymore. Food must, first and foremost, provide fuel for the cells, tickle the senses, and stimulate body and soul.

How to use this book

RECIPES

- All recipes are for 2 to 4 people, depending on how hungry you are. This means that the portion sizes are an approximation, so you can adjust the amount according to your appetite.
- Baking and roasting times for the recipes are only for guidance, so always take a look at the food as you go and adjust the time to meet your desired flavor and texture.
- Taste the food so it suits your particular preference.

INGREDIENTS AND RAW MATERIALS

- I use organic vegetables and ingredients when possible, so the size of special vegetables may vary slightly. Be aware of this.
- All vegetables should be pre-cleaned before being used.
- All recipes are consciously free of gluten, refined sugar, and cow's milk products, as much as possible. In some recipes, though, I've chosen the rich flavor of cream from cow's milk, because I haven't been able to find an equally good plant-based alternative. You can also always choose to use other types of flour or cow's milk products instead of the plant-based varieties in the recipes, if you wish.
- The herbs, plants, and roots in this book can be used fresh, dried, or extracts.

WORTH KNOWING

It can be a good idea to soak nuts, kernels, seeds, beans, and legumes because they contain antinutrients like phytic acid, lectins, tannins, and alpha-galactosidase, which inhibit the human ability to digest and absorb vitamins and minerals. These substances protect the plants against damage from insects and premature germination, but they also inhibit the digestive enzymes in our gut. This means that we have a difficult time absorbing important nutrients like iron, zinc, magnesium, chromium, and manganese from foods that contain antinutrients.

Soak nuts, kernels, seeds, beans, and legumes in tempered water in a ratio of 2:1 (2 parts water to 1 part raw material) with a cloth over them, then drain and rinse the raw material thoroughly until the water runs clear in the sink. Soaked nuts are still crunchy, but if you want them crunchier, you can dry them in your oven at the lowest possible temperature.

RAW MATERIAL	SOAKING TIME	COOKING TIME	DRYING TIME
Nuts in general	8–12 hours		12–24 hours 120°F (50°C)
Cashews	2–6 hours		
Macadamia nuts	2–6 hours		
Walnuts	2–6 hours		
Lentils	2–6 hours		
Kernels in general	8–12 hours		12–20 hours 120°F (50°C)
Pine nuts	2–4 hours		
Beans	12–24 hours	30–60 minutes Add about 1 tablespoon lemon juice or apple cider vinegar for every 2 cups (half liter) beans	
Legumes	12–24 hours		
Seeds in general	5–8 hours		6–12 hours 120°F (50°C)
Chia seeds	2–6 hours		
Flaxseed	1 hour		

GOOD KITCHEN UTENSILS

- Food processor for chopping, blending, kneading, and cutting in no time. Most often, a food processor today also comes with many different attachments, which is extremely practical.
- Powerful blender for making smoothies, dressings, soups, and dips with a delicious, creamy texture. There are big differences between blenders, so I recommend investing in one with a powerful motor.
- A digital kitchen scale is especially useful for measuring flour types and quantities.
- Slow juicer to transform fruit and vegetables into beautiful and luscious juice. Juicers take some time to clean, but they're worth all the trouble.
- A mortar and pestle or coffee grinder to grind spices, seeds, and nuts if your blender or food processor can't do the job. Freshly ground raw materials have a more intense flavor than prepurchased ones.

My pantry

My kitchen supply is neither carefully organized nor orderly, but there are a number of staples that always return to my pantry. These food items are categorized and set up in a clear guide below. You don't need to have all of these materials in your own pantry all at once, but a few ingredients from each category will make it much easier for you to dive into the recipes in this book or conjure up your own creations in no time. Find out what ingredients work best for you and don't get overwhelmed by the whole guide. It is just for inspiration.

You can buy most of the ingredients in your typical supermarket, and you can find the rest in your local health food store or online.

OIL, BUTTER, VINEGAR, AND SAUCES

Good-quality refined oils are an essential part of a pantry, and it matters to our well-being what types of fats and oils are chosen and how they are consumed. Oils are often refined to give them a longer shelf life and make them stable at higher temperatures, but they often lose flavor, aroma, and important nutrients when repeatedly exposed to heat. Unrefined, high-quality fats, on the other hand, help to stabilize blood sugar, give the feeling of satiety, and help the body absorb and use the fat-soluble vitamins in the food.

Naturally fermented, unpasteurized, and unfiltered vinegars are also an indispensable part of the kitchen collection. If you add vinegar to a bean dish or other heavier dishes at the end of cooking, you can perk up the dish and balance the flavors. Traditionally, brewed vinegar has several good properties for both the body's inside and outside. High-quality vinegar contains amino acids and trace minerals and also facilitates digestion and cleansing.

There are countless oils and vinegars on the market, and it can be confusing to find the right kinds on the supermarket shelves. Look for the words "unrefined"

and "extra virgin," and know that you can easily make do with one of each in your everyday cooking.

Apple Cider Vinegar

Apple cider vinegar is a real everyday classic and probably my favorite vinegar. It is light, fresh, fruity, and acidic, and it can be used in everything from dressings to hot, cooked dishes. It is also usually cheaper than many of the other vinegars and has a wide range of health benefits.

Balsamic Vinegar

Red balsamic is good for giving depth to dishes with its light sweet and sour flavor. For example, try adding a bit to tomato-based dishes and caramelized onions, or drizzle it over cheese and desserts. When buying a balsamic, be sure it doesn't contain thickeners or dyes. White balsamic is lighter and sweeter than its red cousin, which makes it perfect for dishes where you don't want the color or the flavor to dominate the dish.

Cocoa Butter

Cocoa butter has a rich and delicate chocolate aroma. You can use cocoa butter in smoothies, ice cream, desserts, and different chocolate creations.

Coconut Butter

Coconut butter contains both the meat and oil of the coconut. You can make your own coconut butter by blending dried coconut the same way you make nut butter. It tastes delicious in different types of breakfast dishes or smoothies, as well as in hot tea and coffee.

Coconut Oil

Coconut oil is known for its antioxidant and antibacterial properties. Coconut oil is one of the only oils that is not destroyed by heating. It is a good butter substitute, especially in baked goods and desserts. It is available both with and without flavor, and if you choose it with flavor, it is sweet and slightly coconut-like. Coconut oil is fluid or creamy at room temperature and firm when refrigerated. You can melt the oil over a water bath or take a quantity and let it melt, for example, on the pan or in the pot where you'll use it.

Flaxseed Oil

Flaxseed oil has a sweet, nutty flavor and tastes delicious drizzled over vegetables, open-faced toast, and salad. I use it mostly in smoothies. It is rich in omega-3 fatty acids and omega-6 fatty acids.

Ghee

Ghee is clarified butter that can be used in both sweet and savory cooking. Its high smoke point makes it perfect for frying.

Miso

Miso is a soft paste made from fermented beans or grains, most commonly soybeans and rice. Unpasteurized miso contains a lot of good probiotic bacteria (like all naturally fermented foods), which strengthens a healthy bacterial flora, digestion, and fat burning. Miso's rich and unique flavor is great for sauces, Asian soups, and stews. Buy organic and GMO-free miso as much as possible.

Olive Oil

Olive oil has a rich, fruity flavor and can be used in everything from dressings to desserts. It can handle frying and baking with low heat. Toss vegetables with it before baking them in the oven, or drizzle it over your salad or pizza.

Rice Wine Vinegar

Traditionally brewed rice wine vinegar has a mild and sweet flavor that is frequently used in Asian dishes. It is also refreshing in pasta dishes, salads, and tofu creations.

Sesame Oil

Sesame oil is a distinct, fragrant, and flavorful oil that adds an intense sesame flavor to dressings, marinades, and vegetables. The oil is especially delicious as a flavor enhancer in Asian dishes. A little of this potent oil goes a long way, so taste as you go.

Soy Sauce and Tamari

Soy sauce and tamari are two of my most used sauces brewed from beans and grains. The flavor of umami is delicious in everyday cooking, especially in vegetable and bean dishes, where it gives the dish depth and richness. Buy organic and GMO-free varieties as much as possible.

Walnut Oil

Walnut oil has a sweet and rounded flavor of nuts. It is not as well known as the other oils, but that certainly does not make it any less delicious. The special flavor of walnuts pairs exceptionally well with baked goods, desserts, and salads—especially with arugula—where it can be allowed to make its mark, but also try playing with it in pasta dishes, sauces, and dressings.

White Wine Vinegar

This type of vinegar has a nice balance between sweetness and acidity. In addition to being an obvious choice to use in marinades and dressings, it is also a fresh addition to salads and light, green summer dishes.

NUTS, KERNELS, AND SEEDS

A pantry is not complete without a good selection of nuts and kernels. They not only enrich everyday meals, snacks, and sweets, but also are rich in protein and good fatty acids. If you buy your nuts completely raw and untreated, you can decide for yourself whether you want to make milk or prepare them another way. If you have space, you can store your nuts and seeds that you don't use regularly in the refrigerator or freezer to prolong freshness.

Almonds

Almonds are rich in healthy fats, vitamins, and minerals. The sweet, marzipan-like flavor of almonds comes out best if you dry-roast them in a pan.

Amaranth (Regular and Puffed)

Like quinoa, amaranth is a grain with a sweet and nutty flavor and an enchanting aroma. It's good both in porridge and as an accompaniment to things like salads, and when it's popped the same way as popcorn.

Brazil Nuts

These oblong nuts are rich in selenium, a mineral that helps balance hormones,

strengthen skin and hair, and protect cells from free radicals, which are chemically unstable molecules with harmful effects on the body. The rich flavor and creamy texture make them delicious in baked goods, as the foundation stone in your favorite muesli, or simply as a small afternoon snack.

Buckwheat Kernels

Buckwheat is a gluten-free type of seed, although the name suggests otherwise. The flavor is mild and becomes nutty when the buckwheat kernels have been in the pan for a while. You can cook them for a delicious breakfast porridge or include them in dishes where you would normally use pasta, couscous, or rice.

Cashews

This slightly curled nut is both sweet and rich. These nuts are especially good as a base for creamy spreads, sweet creams, dressings, or similar.

Chia Seeds

A superseed with the second highest content of omega-3 fatty acids, second only to flaxseed. One of the most easily digestible proteins and a good source of amino acids, minerals, and antioxidants. Chia seeds are eaten raw after they have been soaked to "bloom." They grow and thicken no matter what liquid you put them in, and they can be the base for everything from breakfast to dessert.

Coconut Flour and Flakes
Both flour and flakes are good in breakfast food, baked goods, smoothies, stews, and soups.

Flaxseed
Flaxseed is the seed with the highest content of vegetable omega-3 fatty acids that we know of. The seeds ideally should be ground in order for their nutrients to be absorbed. The flavor is nutty, and flaxseed is delicious in porridge, granola, fruit salads, or vegetable dishes. Whole flaxseed can be soaked overnight in water and added to smoothies to give them a thicker consistency and a nutritional boost. Ground flaxseed can also be mixed with water and used instead of an egg in baking.

Hazelnuts
The small, round nuts with a firm crunch are good both in the sweet kitchen in cakes and creams, and in the savory kitchen as a sprinkle on salads with, for example, cauliflower, leafy greens, and apples.

Hemp Seeds
Hulled hemp seeds are rich in digestion-friendly proteins and contain a wide range of vitamins and minerals. Hemp seeds have a mild, sweet, and nutty flavor that complements both sweet and savory dishes. Sprinkle them over your daily breakfast food, blend them into smoothies, or garnish salads with them.

Nut and Seed Butter
I love nut butter and it's my go-to snack when I often just need a little sweet and salty at the same time. I use it as a spread, in my breakfast porridge or smoothie, on banana slices, in cake, baked goods, and dips. You can easily make your own nut and seed butter by blending your choice of nuts and seeds until smooth and adding a pinch of salt. My favorites are peanut butter, almond butter, tahini (sesame butter), hazelnut butter, and sunflower butter.

Peanuts
In the botanical sense, the peanut is actually not a nut, but a legume that ripens under the ground. Whether peanuts are raw, roasted, or something else entirely, they can be used in a multitude of dishes, or simply eaten as a snack.

They are delicious as creamy nut milk, as a base in sweets and nut butter, or chopped and topped over a crisp salad.

Pine Nuts
Pine nuts are small, oblong, white seeds with a sweet and sharp flavor. Pine

nuts are usually toasted in a pan before use, and they can be used in numerous contexts: in salads, pesto, cakes, and as a snack.

Pistachios

The nut with the changing green and pink color adds effortless beauty to any sweet or savory dish. Pistachios taste mild and delicately perfumed, and after a light toasting in the pan, they are wonderful for spicing up an ordinary, everyday dish.

Psyllium Husks

Psyllium husks are small, fiber-containing flakes with a good ability to bind moisture and flour together, so bread and baked goods get a moister texture and become springier and airier.

Pumpkin Seeds

Pumpkin seeds have a satisfying, nutty flavor without being too dominant. Lightly toast them until they're golden and crispy and sprinkle them over beans, legumes, and salad, or let them be part of a delicious granola. They're a good source of omega-3 fatty acids, zinc, and iron.

Quinoa (Regular and Puffed)

Quinoa is one of my favorite seeds. They are rich in nutrients and contain more calcium than milk, as well as all nine amino acids, so they're a very good source of protein. They're easy to prepare and have a light texture and a mild, nutty flavor that works well in both the sweet and savory kitchen.

Sesame

Sesame seeds are rich in protein and a good source of calcium and iron. They have a nutty flavor that's brought out more clearly if you toast them in a pan. They can be used in seed milk, as a topping on dishes, in tahini, or in dressings.

Sunflower

Sunflower seeds can be used in seed milk, pesto, and baked goods, sprinkled over salads, or stirred into porridge. If you toast them in a pan, the sweet flavor is accentuated, and the crispy shell provides a perfect counterpoint to soft dishes. The seeds are also a good source of calcium and iron.

Walnuts

Walnuts are rich in omega-3 fatty acids, which support brain function and can help reduce inflammation. The walnut is a fatty nut, which makes it good for pesto and nut butter. After a trip to the pan, where the walnuts are lightly toasted, they're also wonderful as a topping on salads, in baked goods, or desserts.

Yeast Flakes

Yeast flakes are neither a nut nor a seed, but deactivated yeast. It cannot be used as a leavening agent, but instead, the flakes are delicious sprinkled over salad and pasta dishes or added to sauce. The flavor is cheesy and mild and satisfies the desire for umami.

BEANS AND LEGUMES

Beans and legumes are the green kitchen's number one protein source, and they're rich in fiber, vitamins, minerals, and complex carbohydrates. The flavor of home-cooked beans and legumes will always surpass those you can buy canned, but sometimes it can be nice to have a few cans in stock to whip up a dip or bean paste quickly. I hope that more beans and legumes will find their way into your favorite dishes, because they're satisfying, inexpensive, and better for our planet.

Beluga Lentils

These beautiful, shiny, black lentils add a wonderful touch to a salad. Their firmness makes them hold their shape better than red and yellow lentils and not get mushy as easily. They're a great alternative to rice or pasta and also work well in a mash or soup.

Black Beans

Black beans have a mild flavor and are great in soups and stews, and partly mashed for a simple sauce in dishes.

When cooked, black beans retain a firm but creamy texture that also makes them suitable for use as a substitute for flour in, for example, chocolate cake.

Borlotti Beans

Borlotti beans are small and mild beans that are especially good in pâtés and mash, since they don't become floury when you mash them. They're also a good alternative to chickpeas in stews.

Butter Beans

Butter beans are large, flat, white beans that can be prepared relatively quickly and get a soft and creamy texture. This makes them perfect in a tossed salad, one-pot dishes, or for making soup.

Cannellini Beans

Smaller than lima beans, but still full of flavor and texture. After cooking, they become creamy, which makes them ideal for spreads or dips.

Chickpeas

Chickpeas are my favorite legume and a good substitute for meat. During preparation, they will become creamy and take on a nutty flavor. They contain more iron and vitamin C than any other bean or legume. Mash them into a rough look-alike scramble, marinate them, or blend them into a rich and luscious hummus, and let them elevate your salad and other dishes.

Edamame Beans

Elegant, green soybeans with a firm texture and rich in protein. They're delicious in dishes and salad bowls.

Kidney Beans

With its deep red color and kidney-shaped appearance, the kidney bean is a sweet, luscious, and creamy bean, which makes it perfect for spicy dishes and marinating, as it holds both shape and flavor well.

Lentils (Red, Yellow, and Green)

Lentils are quick to prepare and soften easily in no time, making them formidable in quick soups, a dhal, or one-pot dishes that require a bit of richness. The flavor is neutral and they work with all kinds of spices and herbs, so don't be afraid to dive into using lentils in your cooking.

Mung Beans

The olive green color is beautiful and breathtaking, and these spectacular beans are easy to prepare. Their texture and nutty flavor work well in hot stews like dahl, in salads, and as a component in a bean pâté.

Tofu

Tofu is made from fermented soybeans and can be used in both cold and hot dishes. With breading, marinade, or spices, you can conjure almost anything out of tofu. Buy GMO-free tofu as much as possible.

PLANT MILK AND CREAM

Milk can seem almost indispensable in cooking, and fortunately, the selection of plant-based alternatives to cow's milk has gradually grown in supermarkets. However, there's a big difference in the quality, so please read the ingredients list to make sure the drink isn't filled with a lot of sugar and unnecessary additives. You can also easily make your own plant milk yourself by blending nuts or seeds with water and filtering the drink in a nut milk bag if you want it fine. The ratio is about 1:3 of nuts, seeds, or kernels to water, but try it out and adjust for the flavor and texture you want. The milk can easily last 4–5 days in the fridge.

Coconut Milk

Coconut milk is a plant oil–based milk that is frequently used in Indian and Asian dishes. The fatty part, especially, which tastes sweet and coconut-like, is also delicious to use in ice cream, desserts, and smoothies. Choose the kind with the highest fat content, as this variety is usually the least refined and also tastes the best.

Cream (oat, soy, rice, and nut)

Plant-based cream is an incredibly good alternative to cream made from cow's

milk. There are many excellent, ready-made varieties in the supermarkets.

Hemp Milk

Hemp milk is sweet, and the homemade variety tastes much better than the purchased one, which can taste a little bitter. It's especially good in dishes because the flavor is exotic and tones down strong spices. Pancakes can also get a lovely, sweet touch with this milk.

Nut Milk

Milk made from nuts is often creamy and sweet, which makes it extremely useful in the sweet kitchen or as a base for chocolate milk or a warm latte.

Oat Milk

Probably the milk I use most often, since it's one of the least expensive varieties of plant milk you can both make and buy. The flavor is sweet, and the milk is delicious both cold and hot, so you can use it in porridge and coffee, or pour it over your breakfast food, since it doesn't separate.

Rice Milk

Rice milk is slightly sweeter than oat milk and works especially well in smoothies, breakfast foods, and desserts.

Seed Milk

You can easily make milk from seeds. Hemp seeds, sunflower seeds, and pumpkin seeds, especially, lend a delicious flavor.

Soy Milk

Probably the milk that most resembles regular cow's milk. It works well for cooking, baked goods, and in coffee.

FLOUR, GRAIN, AND BAKED GOODS

There is nothing quite like the smell and flavor of freshly baked buns, bread, or cakes. Something that can arouse the joy of anticipation and bring a smile to most people's lips, even on gray and boring days. For me, the smell of home baking often evokes memories of my grandmother's white French bread with a crunchy crust, and her kringle (danishes), of which I could easily devour several pieces at a time.

Home baking has become a particularly high-priority and very stress-relieving discipline, where everything from advanced kneading techniques to new flour compositions are tested. If you haven't already jumped on the bandwagon, I would strongly recommend that you start baking, yourself. Here is a list of the gluten-free flour types I use most often, so you can reap all the good benefits of home baking.

Almond Flour

One of the most delicious nut-based types of flour that fits well in the sweet kitchen, and especially shortcrust pastry and piecrusts. This flour has a high fat content and characteristic texture. You can buy it ready-made or easily make it yourself by grinding or blending whole almonds in a food processor.

Baking Powder

If you don't use yeast, baking powder is indispensable in muffins, bread, and cakes that need to rise.

Buckwheat Flour

This type of flour is sweet and rich and probably the kind I use most often. Despite the name, buckwheat flour has nothing to do with wheat. It is transformed into everything from pancakes and bread to desserts and cakes. This type of flour is distinctive and helps to create cohesion and strength in dough. It is often mixed with other, lighter types of flour like rice flour, corn flour, and similar.

Cassava Flour

Cassava flour is very similar to wheat flour in flavor and texture and can be used as a substitute in most recipes without any unpleasant surprises. Cassava is a delicious root vegetable that, when dried and ground, makes a nice alternative to wheat.

Chestnut Flour

A more expensive type of flour, but the sweet and nutty flavor outweighs the price. Like many of the other types of flour, it's good in both baked goods and cakes.

Chickpea Flour

A good, versatile type of flour with a high content of fiber and protein that works well with almond flour in pie dough and shortcrust pastry, as well as crêpes and pizza crust. The flavor is slightly nutty.

Chufa Flour

Chufa, which is also known as earth almonds or tiger nuts, is actually neither an almond nor a nut, but a small tuber that grows underground in southern countries, and it has been known and used for thousands of years. The taste is sweet and coconutty, which makes chufa flour an obvious choice for use in baked goods, piecrusts, cookies, and cakes. It can also be replaced 1:1 with almond flour or mixed with other types of flour. In addition, chufa has good fiber content, so it's good for digestion.

Coconut Flour

Coconut flour has a high content of dietary fiber and protein. This flour can be used as an alternative to almond flour in bread and cakes, to thicken sauce, or as a sprinkle of fiber on your breakfast smoothie or porridge.

Cornmeal

Cornmeal is made from ground corn kernels and has a strong flavor of sweet corn. Really delicious in tortillas, cornbread, polenta, or muffins.

Cornstarch

Cornstarch is starch made from the inner part of corn kernels. Cornstarch is good for thickening dishes and in baking.

Millet Flour

Millet flour has a light texture and a high protein and fiber content. The flavor is sweet, and millet flour is used mainly for baked goods and desserts, where it's often combined with other flour to prevent the baked goods from crumbling.

Quinoa Flour

A type of flour rich in protein that makes baked goods moist. Quinoa flour can be used for everything from baking bread and cakes to other substitutes for the traditional types of grain.

Rolled Oats and Oat Flour

These beautiful flakes are used in porridge, buns, pancakes, and cookies. You can easily make your own oat flour by grinding or blending the meal in a food processor. Otherwise, oat flour is also available in most major supermarkets.

Tapioca Flour

Tapioca flour is extracted from the roots of the cassava plant and is slightly similar to potato flour, so it's a good gluten-free alternative for thickening sauces and soups, breading, and in baking in general, where it binds the dough together. However, this type of flour must not be confused with cassava flour, even though both types of flour originate from the same tuber. It is the production process that distinguishes these two types of flour.

Teff Flour

Teff is a kind of grass with very small seeds. Similar to chufa flour, this type of flour also has a nutty flavor. Use teff flour across the kitchen, where it does well in sweeter baked goods, like bread, cakes, pancakes, and porridge.

Whole-Grain Rice Flour

Whole-grain rice flour has a nutty flavor and is good as a base in baked goods together with other types of flour.

Xanthan Gum

Xanthan gum is a gelling and thickening agent used especially in gluten-free baking for improving the crumb structure. By binding oil and water, it makes the bread firmer so it doesn't crumble as easily. In addition, xanthan gum also prevents the formation of ice crystals, so it is good to use if you want to make homemade ice cream. If you want extra creamy dressings, mayonnaise, and ice cream, you can also use xanthan gum for that.

Yeast (Fresh and Dried)

Classic element in many baked goods. However, dry yeast is easier to store than fresh yeast, so always make sure you have a bag in the cupboard so you can easily whip up a ball of dough.

PASTA AND NOODLES

Pasta and noodles come in many shapes, sizes, and varieties. I don't eat wheat pasta or other gluten-containing varieties, myself, but fortunately, there are a multitude of alternatives that are more nutritious and taste better.

Bean and Lentil Pasta

Pasta made with chickpeas, lentils, or beans is my favorite pasta in simple, everyday dishes and more complex weekend dishes. They are all rich in protein, and the carbohydrate content is lower than in traditional wheat pasta.

Buckwheat Noodles (Soba Noodles)

They resemble thin spaghetti but are darker than regular wheat pasta. These noodles are versatile and can be used in everything from hot soups and wok dishes in the winter to cold salads in the summer. The flavor is slightly nutty, and the texture is firm.

Kelp Noodles

Kelp is a vegetable from under the surface of the sea. It is known by some as seaweed and can be made into raw-food noodles. The texture is a bit firm and kelp noodles don't have much flavor, but with a dressing or sauce, they can be spiced up easily.

Shirataki Noodles

These noodles are made from the konjac root and are a brilliant alternative to regular pasta. They can be used in dishes where you would normally use wheat pasta, and hold their consistency well.

Vegetable Spaghetti

Vegetable spaghetti is an easy way to get more vegetables in. You can make spaghetti from many different kinds of vegetables with a spiralizer or a potato peeler. I particularly like squash, carrots, Chinese radish, cabbage, and pumpkin.

HEALTHIER, NATURAL SWEETENERS

The deep and complex flavor of natural sweeteners is far more interesting and satisfying than white sugar and other artificial sweeteners that have been stripped of all vitamins and nutrients. These naturally sweet raw materials each contribute their own flavor, character, and texture, and it can be an art to find the right composition, so try them out yourself and find your favorites.

Apple Syrup, Apple Juice, and Unsweetened Applesauce

The sweet flavor of apples is a good alternative to bananas and dates in cooking. A good applesauce can hold granola and baked goods together, while a juice can perk up juices and other cold drinks.

Bananas

Bananas sweeten in an understated way and are good in smoothies, bread, cookies, and baked goods. They fill you up well and are rich in potassium and fiber.

Coconut Palm Syrup and Coconut Sugar

Coconut palm syrup is extracted by tapping the flower sap of the coconut palm, which is then evaporated and boiled so it turns into a thick syrup. If the syrup is evaporated further, the mass can be ground and turned into coconut sugar. Coconut palm syrup and coconut sugar do not affect blood sugar to the same degree as other sweeteners, and contain amino acids, minerals, and B vitamins. The flavor is mild and slightly caramelly. If you're used to eating regular sugar, you will probably discover that coconut sugar and coconut syrup are less sweet. You can use coconut sugar in pretty much any recipe where you would normally use regular sugar.

Dates and Date Syrup

Dates are perfect for sweetening smoothies and plant milk. Together with nuts, they also work as a good base in truffles, cakes, and piecrusts. Their sweet and tender flesh adds character and a rich, caramelly flavor without being overwhelming. Date syrup is an excellent alternative to honey and maple syrup.

Honey

Honey is bursting with antioxidants, vitamins, and minerals, and deliciously sweetens tea and cakes. Since the flavor is sweeter than regular white sugar, you can often be satisfied with less honey in baking recipes and desserts.

Maple Syrup

Maple syrup is tapped from the maple tree and has a rich, dark, and sweet caramelized flavor. Maple syrup is a good substitute for regular sugar and tastes excellent on protein-rich porridge, in sweet baked goods, and in savory snacks.

Vanilla

Good-quality vanilla is, along with saffron, the most expensive spice available. With its delicate floral aroma and unique flavor, it is undoubtedly my favorite spice in nut milk and all kinds of desserts.

Introduction and guide to nature's wild pantry

HERBS, PLANTS, AND ROOTS IN GENERAL

Herbs are more than just flavoring agents and garnishes in a dish. Along with thousands of other roots, stems, and fruits, they are also full of natural vitamins and minerals that help create the foundation for a healthy and vital life. We can learn as much from bringing plants into our kitchen as our predecessors have done for millennia.

There is nothing like the aroma and flavor of fresh plants and herbs, and in most cases, I would go for the fresh kind, if it makes sense in relation to the dish I'm making. Dried herbs or oils are not necessarily the next best thing. They are practical, keep for a long time, and in some cases, I prefer the dried version of an herb to the fresh one. Some people are reluctant when buying fresh herbs because they either don't know what to use them for, what foods they interact

with, or simply think it's a waste of money. I hope I can help inspire you to use more herbs in your cooking, whether they're fresh, dried, or extracted as oils, and show you that it doesn't need to be complicated, require a lot of knowledge of herbs, or, for that matter, be a waste of money.

PURCHASE AND STORAGE OF FRESH HERBS

If you can, buy dried aromatic herbs whole and grind them yourself. It requires a bit more work, but the flavor is also more intense and uplifting. When shopping for fresh herbs, look for vibrant colors and fresh aromas. Avoid leaves that are damaged, yellow, or have brown spots. You can buy the fresh ones loose, in packages, or as plants. Having herb plants in your home allows you to simply cut off the amount you need, and the rest of the plant will continue growing for several months.

You can store your fresh herbs in the refrigerator for several days by removing any rubber bands and immersing the stems in a glass with 1¼ to 1½ inches of water. If the herbs wilt, you can cut a couple of inches off the stems and place them in a glass of ice water for a few hours to bring them back to life.

USE OF HERBS IN COOKING
Wash your herbs right when you're ready to use them. To loosen dirt, you can rinse them under the faucet or place them in a bowl of cold water and gently push them around, then dry them in a salad spinner or by dabbing them with a dish towel. You can chop your herbs with a knife or cut them with kitchen scissors. Chop the herbs right before using them in your dish so they stay fresh for as long as possible.

If the herbs are to be used as an aromatic background flavor in your dish, add them at the beginning of your cooking, usually right after heating the oil or preparing the first few ingredients, like onions. You can add whole sprigs of an herb to your pot or pan, then remove them when the food is done. Dried herbs should also be added early in the recipe so the flavor is released into the food. If you want to use the flavor of the fresh herbs to the fullest, you should chop them and add them at the end of the recipe. And, obviously, herbs are the perfect garnish to top off your culinary masterpiece.

If you have aromatic herbs left over, you can easily blend them together with a good-quality oil, and in a snap, you have an herbal oil ready for use. You can also dry the aromatic herbs and grind them in a mortar and pestle with salt to create an extra fresh zest for cooking at your fingertips.

ADAPTOGENIC HERBS
Our body is incredibly resilient and has a very special ability to adapt to many different conditions, but it can have difficulty handling everything it encounters without proper nutrition and physiological support. Many are challenged by stress and extreme fatigue, which can profoundly affect our mental health and quality of life. Chronically elevated cortisol levels can affect any system in the body, such as overworked adrenal glands, a challenged digestive tract, rapid aging, anxiety, chronic fatigue, hormone imbalances, and much more. In such cases, adaptogens can be a dear friend.

Adaptogens are a group of powerful and potent plants and mushrooms that behave a bit differently than other herbs. For hundreds of years, they have been used in herbal medical practice, particularly within Chinese medicine and Ayurveda, to increase the body's strength, endurance, and resilience. They got their name because of their unique ability to normalize and balance the body's functions in the individual person, as the active ingredients of the herbs enter and support the body's and the brain's ability to adapt and thus increase the body's resilience in connection with physical, psychological, and/or chemical stress. This means that the adaptogens do not intervene disruptively when the body functions normally and optimally.

An adaptogen therefore does not have a specific function, nor can it target a specific part of the body or a particular challenge. Instead, the individual herb or mushroom works in a balanced field of tension, being able to both stimulate and inhibit bodily functions, mentally, physically, and emotionally, depending on the need at the given time. The explanation for this paradox is that adaptogens influence the brain's overall regulatory system, the hormone system, and the immune system.

HOW DO ADAPTOGENS WORK?

Adaptogens work specifically with the immune system, the endocrine system, and the neuroendocrine system. This means that the adaptogenic herbs increase the ability of the cells to both form and develop energy in stressful situations, whether it's acute, chronic, or psychological stress. When the cells have access to more energy, the oxygen in the body is used more efficiently and it becomes easier to excrete waste products. In addition, the antioxidative properties of adaptogens help to protect against the harmful effects of free radicals.

Adaptogens do not cause side effects and are also not addictive.

HOW TO TAKE ADAPTOGENS

Adaptogens can be taken in many different ways, and there are powders, pills or capsules, and liquid extracts. Extracts are great if you prefer regular tea or often have them on the go. Powder works best if blended or mixed with other wet ingredients, since it can clump.

Below, you will find a small overview of which forms, in addition to the fresh and dried varieties, these magical plants are available as:

Extract and Tincture

Tinctures consist of an alcohol base and are more concentrated and potent than teas or decoctions. They can be mixed into hot and cold drinks or simply dripped under the tongue, although the flavor may be sharp.

Powder

Powder is made from dried raw ingredients that are ground. Powder is versatile and easy to work with. It can be mixed into your daily tea, smoothies, or used in cooking.

Capsules

Capsules consist of a dried raw ingredient in a vegetable capsule that makes them easy to consume. Capsules are useful when you are traveling or if you have difficulty consuming tincture or powder.

Decoction or Infusion

Tea made from either fresh or dried raw ingredients that have steeped for several hours. The longer you let your ingredient steep, the stronger and more concentrated your drink will be.

Elixir

An alcoholic drink made from a mixture of different herbs and honey to sweeten it a bit. Can be used in the same way as extracts and tinctures.

If this is your first time taking adaptogens, I would suggest that you start out slowly by incorporating two to three different kinds into your daily routine. Start by consuming them individually, for example in a superfood latte, so you feel the effect each adaptogen has on your body and mind.

Also, be patient. You don't necessarily feel the effect right away, as it's not a quick fix. Allow the adaptogens to adjust their effects to your body over a period of two to three weeks or longer, where you take the adaptogen daily with a healthy diet, so you can observe the energy of the adaptogen you are taking. In contrast to conventional medicinal preparations, the herbs work more holistically and over a longer period, so patience, time, and continuity are the alpha and omega if you want to reap the full effect of the individual adaptogen.

You can mix your adaptogens into lattes, smoothies, and tea, bake them into cakes and sweets, or sprinkle them on porridge and yogurt. The possibilities are limited only by your imagination. Try to combine them with healthy fats like coconut oil, flaxseed oil, or similar, since this is the best way to metabolize them. Dosage can vary depending on which herb it is, how it is extracted, and what it is used for. With these powerful plants, more is not necessarily better. Therefore, use them with care and specifically choose the ones that suit your needs. If you are a novice, start out with less than the recommended dose. Try dosing with ⅛ to ¼ teaspoon powdered adaptogen, and slowly work your way up to ½ to 1 teaspoon, which is a general rule of thumb for dosage if you are taking adaptogens on a daily basis. Preferably take adaptogens two to three times during the day.

In this context, pay attention to what time of day you take the individual adaptogen. Some adaptogens can work better in the morning than in the evening, but this is a very individual assessment. For example, reishi can be deeply calming for most people, while for others it can increase energy levels. Other adaptogens such as rhodiola are more stimulating and invigorating and are therefore taken by many first thing in the day.

If you take adaptogens daily, you should take periodic breaks. Some research suggests that these breaks also improve the ability of adaptogens to work. Generally, a pattern of three weeks of intake and one week off is recommended. Also, preferably rotate between the different adaptogens in this cycle.

There are also delicious, ready-made matcha and cocoa mixes, where the proportions have already been carefully measured and you know the ingredients are of high quality.

Last but not least, it is also important to be aware that certain adaptogenic herbs should not be consumed by children, pregnant women, or anyone with heart problems. Since herbal remedies and dietary supplements can affect possible treatment with other medications, you should always consult your doctor first if you are taking prescription medication.

The properties that appear in the following herb guide are suggestions for how you can use nature's toolbox to support a body and mind in balance.

Herb Guide

AÇAI

Flavor: Chocolate and blackberry-like.
Use: This beautiful purple-red powder comes from a small berry from South America, and I use it most often in my smoothies or if I want to color cakes or bread.
Properties:

- Rich in antioxidants
- May have a moisturizing and repairing effect
- Contributes to a well-functioning digestive system
- Good for fatigue and exhaustion

Hallmarks: Energizing and moisturizing.

ALLSPICE

Taste: Spicy and aromatic.
Use: The berries (whole or ground) are often used in sauces and stews as a flavor enhancer of other spices. You probably also know it from Christmas baking, where it contributes a warm, spicy aroma, so it's quite delicious in bread and sweet baked goods like cakes, cookies, and muffins.
Properties:

- Can relieve intestinal and stomach discomfort as well as muscle pain
- Contributes to a feeling of warmth in the body
- Can have an inhibitory effect on bacteria and fungi in the body
- Has antioxidant properties
- Supports a healthy cardiovascular and circulatory system

Hallmarks: Stimulates digestion and relief.

AMLA

Flavor: Fresh, astringent, and slightly acidic.
Use: Amla powder is especially good in warm lattes, but can also be stirred into your plant milk, smoothie, yogurt, or juice. The slightly acidic flavor also works well in breakfast dishes, desserts, or salads.
Properties:

- A helping hand for colds and flu-like symptoms
- Strengthens the skin and hair
- Positive influence on inflammation and the immune system
- Can have a stabilizing effect on connective tissue and blood vessels
- Beneficial for a sensitive gut

Hallmarks: Anti-inflammatory and vitalizing.

ANISE

Flavor: Licorice-like.
Use: Anise can be used in hot and cold drinks, desserts, and dressings.
Properties:

- Helps to support flow in digestion for stomach problems and nausea
- Can have a positive impact on insomnia
- Has a calming and relaxing effect
- Has an expectorant effect
- Freshens breath
- Can help to improve blood circulation in the skin

Hallmarks: Supports digestion.

ASTRAGALUS

Flavor: Sweet and nutty.

Use: In the same way as the other adaptogens, astragalus powder can be stirred into a smoothie, juice, latte, or tea. The adaptogen can also be included in various raw-ball combinations.

Properties:
- Alleviates inflammation in the body
- Strengthens the body's immune system
- Good for fatigue and exhaustion
- Supports a healthy liver
- Can help with a healthy cardiovascular system and increase blood circulation

Hallmarks: Strengthens the immune system.

BASIL

Flavor: Spicy, floral, and a slight hint of anise.

Uses: Basil can be used in everything from pesto, soups, and stews, to salads, sandwiches, and even desserts. It works particularly well with tomatoes and is therefore often used in Italian cuisine.

Properties:
- Plays a positive role for your eyesight and your skin
- Anti-inflammatory and pain-relieving properties
- Supports the blood's transport of oxygen in the body
- Is antibacterial and can therefore be effective against viruses and bacterial infections
- Muscle-relaxing properties that can contribute to a good sleep

Hallmarks: Anti-inflammatory and muscle relaxing.

BAY LEAF

Flavor: Strong and spicy, almost woody.

Use: Bay leaves normally are used in soups, stews, sauces, and other dishes with a longer cooking time. The leaves give the dishes depth and character.

Properties:
- Contributes to relaxing muscles and joints
- Has a positive effect on the immune system
- Can act as an expectorant and relieve blocked airways
- A possible support for a sluggish and hard stomach, bloating, cramps, and gas
- Can calm the mind

Hallmarks: Expectorant and digestion promoting.

BEE POLLEN

Flavor: Strong, bittersweet, and slightly reminiscent of honey.

Use: The small yellow or orange granules are perfect for sprinkling over porridge, desserts, or smoothies. As with honey, flavor and color can vary greatly, depending on which plant your bee pollen comes from.

Properties:
- Filled with proteins, B vitamins, antioxidants, and amino acids
- Can contribute to regulating gut bacteria and neutralizing toxic waste materials
- Promotes healthy digestion
- Is energizing
- Can have a positive influence on the treatment of addiction problems
- Contributes to the relief of allergies

Hallmarks: Uplifting and anti-inflammatory.

BURDOCK ROOT

Flavor: Earthy and dry.

Use: In addition to being suitable for teas and tinctures, burdock root is also surprisingly useful either boiled, roasted, fried, or baked along with other vegetables and in a delicious dip, salad, or soup.

Properties:
- Can be effective with anti-inflammatory conditions
- Can act as a blood purifier
- Good for skin problems like rashes and skin impurities
- Has diuretic and detoxifying properties

Hallmarks: Cleansing and detoxifying.

CALENDULA

Flavor: Mild and slightly spicy.

Use: Calendula can be used in a myriad of ways in the kitchen. The petals are beautiful as a garnish for desserts, baked goods, and salads, but can also be used in the food itself and in herbal teas.

Properties:
- Has a positive effect on bloating, cramps, and gas
- Supports bile and liver
- A helping hand with inhibiting bacteria, fungal growth, and viruses
- Can heal irritated and inflamed skin such as wounds, rashes, and burns
- Good for inflammation and itching from insect bites

Hallmarks: Anti-inflammatory.

CARDAMOM

Flavor: Sweet and eucalyptus-like.

Use: Cardamom is primarily used in the sweet (Christmas) kitchen in cakes, baked goods, and teas, but is also an important ingredient in, among other things, heavier one-pot dishes.

Properties:
- Good for colds and coughs
- Can have a strengthening effect on the immune system
- Supports balanced digestion and helps relieve bloating
- Can help fight bad breath

Hallmarks: Digestive balancing and immune strengthening.

CAYENNE PEPPER

Flavor: Spicy, bitter, and slightly burning.

Use: The reddish-brown spice is used often in stews, omelets, risotto, and baked goods when a hot and spicy flavor is desired. It can also contribute an extra kick to sauerkraut or tea and tinctures.

Properties:
- Has anti-inflammatory properties
- Can help improve and strengthen blood circulation
- Supports the body's fat burning
- Has a positive influence on the body's appetite regulation and energy level
- Can act as a pain reliever for discomfort, especially in the throat and gastrointestinal system

Hallmarks: Analgesic, stimulating, and anti-inflammatory.

CHAGA

Flavor: Bitter.

Use: Chaga is ideal in teas and lattes, but also tastes delicious in smoothies, yogurt, or in porridge.

Properties:

- Can have an immune-boosting effect
- Has a positive impact on age-related memory loss
- An aid for skin, hair, and digestion
- Contributes to endurance and physical development

Hallmarks: Immune balancing, stimulating, and energizing.

CHAMOMILE

Flavor: Slightly bitter and floral.

Use: Good in tea and lattes but can also be used for a lot more in the kitchen, among other things, in sweet dishes.

- Good for skin problems like eczema, a rash, and irritated eyes

Hallmarks: Soothing and calming.

Properties:

- Can have a relaxing, calming, and slightly sleepy effect
- Has a positive impact on indigestion and stomach bloating
- A possible support for pain relief, especially with muscle and menstrual pain
- Can reduce inflammatory conditions

CHILI

Flavor: Warm and strong.

Use: Chili gives a little kick in everything from soups and stews, to dressings, marinades, and even drinks.

Properties:

- Has antioxidant and cleansing properties
- Supports a healthy gut
- Can increase the feeling of satiety
- Can have a mild local anesthetic effect and be pain relieving

Hallmarks: Cleansing and stimulating.

CHIVE

Flavor: Mild and sharp at the same time.

Use: Like its fellow congeners, onions and garlic, chives are a versatile herb that can do much more than just act as a garnish. Worth highlighting are recipes with potatoes, salads, omelets, and homemade spreadable cheeses.

Properties:

- Is good for digestion
- Can have an appetite-regulating effect
- Has a positive effect on blood pressure
- Can be slightly invigorating

Hallmarks: Promotes digestion.

CHLORELLA

Flavor: Earthy.

Use: This beautiful green algae is easiest to use in either capsule or powder form. If you choose the powder, it can be used in a sea of breakfast recipes, cakes, desserts, smoothies, tea, and wherever else you could think of adding an extra hint of green to.

Properties:

- Rich in amino acids
- Can be used against bad breath and body odor

- Has a positive impact on the immune system
- Can support digestion
- Has detoxifying properties and can help excrete waste from the body

Hallmarks: Detoxifying, cleansing, and strengthening.

CILANTRO

Flavor: Aromatic, slightly bitter, and perfumed.

Use: Cilantro is often used in spicy food and is an indispensable topping on Mexican, Indian, and Asian dishes. This herb gives plenty of flavor and character to marinades, pesto, sauce, and dressings. The stem can be eaten easily, as well, and tastes lovely.

Properties:
- Contributes to lowering high cholesterol levels
- Can counteract bad breath
- Provides care for intestinal discomfort
- Can have a diuretic and cleansing effect
- Good for inflammation
- Has antibacterial properties

Hallmarks: Digestion promoting and detoxifying.

CINNAMON

Flavor: Sweet and warm.

Use: Cinnamon tastes great in baked goods, desserts, breakfast, and tea, but can also work well in savory dishes and heavy stews.

Properties:
- A help with maintaining a healthy blood sugar level

- Has a positive effect on appetite and digestion
- Can have a beneficial influence on your cholesterol
- Has antibacterial properties
- Contributes to general vitality

Hallmarks: Blood sugar stabilizing and antibacterial.

CLOVE

Flavor: Spicy.

Use: With its especially spicy flavor, the clove is one of the most important components in mulled wine. In addition, it does well in cakes and desserts, as well as in winter soups and simmering dishes, where it gives good depth.

Properties:
- Can relieve bloating and eliminate intestinal gas
- Has antibacterial properties and can act as a pain reliever
- Contributes to maintaining good oral hygiene
- Helps fight viruses and bacteria in the throat and lungs

Hallmarks: Promotes digestion and is antibacterial.

COCOA

Flavor: Bitter and sharp or sweet.

Use: One of the most used, but perhaps also the most overlooked superfoods. Enriches everything from desserts and cakes to smoothies and lattes. One can never have too much cocoa.

Properties:
- Loaded with antioxidants

- Can have a positive effect on the heart and circulation
- Is rich in fiber and can help regulate blood sugar and blood pressure

Hallmarks: Mood lifting and anti-inflammatory.

CORDYCEPS

Flavor: Salty, umami, and slightly earthy.
Use: Cordyceps can be mixed with everything from soups to stews or enjoyed in a tea or latte.
Properties:
- Contributes to physical performance and endurance
- Can have a relaxing effect on the lungs and stimulate breathing
- Has a positive influence on sex drive and fertility

Hallmarks: Energizing, performance-enhancing, and mood-lifting.

CUMIN

Flavor: Aromatic, slightly bitter, and woody.
Use: Cumin is particularly delicious in hummus, chili con carne, curries, and garam masala.
Properties:
- Can help to stimulate digestion
- Has anti-inflammatory properties and can relieve inflammation
- Contributes to strengthening the skin and protecting against free radicals
- Has disinfecting properties

Hallmarks: Antibacterial and strengthening.

DANDELION (DANDELION ROOT)

Flavor: Sour and slightly bitter.
Use: Dandelion is good in salads, vegetable dishes, and tea. The leaf rosettes can be used as a garnish in salads and desserts.
Properties:
- May have a pain-relieving effect
- Supports the liver's general health and can have a cleansing effect
- Contributes to stimulating the digestive juices in the stomach
- A helping hand with promoting appetite and supporting digestion (mild laxative)

Hallmarks: Cleansing and fortifying.

DILL

Flavor: Delicate and mild with notes of pepper and licorice.
Use: Dill is delicious in yogurt-based sauces and salads.
Properties:
- Good for a bloated stomach and digestive discomfort
- Can be effective against cold and flu symptoms
- Stimulates internal heat
- Is rich in antioxidants, which can boost the immune system
- Has a high content of iron and calcium, which strengthens bones and teeth

Hallmarks: Strengthens stomach and bones

ECHINACEA

Flavor: Bitter and floral.

Use: Echinacea is often used in water, herbal tea, and other drinks.

Properties:
- Can have a preventive and acute effect on bacteria and viruses
- Contributes to supporting the body's own resistance
- Is rich in antioxidants
- Supports the body's cleansing of the blood and can act stimulating on lymphatic system
- Can have a detoxifying and cleansing effect
- Has a positive effect on skin problems such as rashes, infections, and impure skin

Hallmarks: Antiviral and cleansing.

ELDERFLOWER

Flavor: Sweet and perfumed.

Use: Many people know the flower from the well-known cocktail/mocktail favorite, elderflower liqueur, but these small, beautiful clusters are also delicious in cakes and desserts.

Properties:
- Can reduce fluid retention in the body
- Provides relief for a sore throat
- Can have a soothing effect on inflammatory and viral conditions
- Good for insomnia, nervousness, and depression

Hallmarks: Diuretic and soothing.

FENNEL

Flavor: Slightly sweet licorice flavor.

Use: The leaves add a fresh touch to vegetable dishes, while the seeds are delicious for spicing up warm and cool drinks.

Properties:
- Can stimulate milk production with nursing
- Has a positive impact on digestion and can remedy bad breath
- Has antibacterial properties and can support the body in fighting inflammation
- Contributes to strengthening the hair and preventing hair loss
- Has diuretic properties

Hallmarks: Digestive relieving and antibacterial.

GARLIC

Flavor: Strong and powerful.

Use: In my view, garlic is indispensable in every kitchen and works in virtually all dishes, except the sweet ones.

Properties:
- Has anti-inflammatory properties and can be effective against all kinds of unwanted bacteria, viruses, or fungi
- A possible support for cleansing and removing heavy metals and toxins from the body
- Has a positive impact on high cholesterol

- Can contribute to a supple and healthy blood circulation

Hallmarks: Cleansing and antiviral.

GINGER

Flavor: Spicy, bitter, and sweet.

Use: Ginger is a versatile root and can be used in many ways in various stews and baked goods, as well as in juice, smoothies, tea, marmalades, and compotes.

Properties:

- Can improve digestion
- A helping hand with stomach and intestinal problems
- Contributes to stimulating circulation
- Can relieve pain and stiffness in the body
- Good for feelings of nausea and motion sickness
- Plays a positive role in relation to reducing inflammation and pain

Hallmarks: Anti-inflammatory and stimulating.

GINKGO BILOBA

Flavor: Mild, earthy, and slightly bitter.

Use: This powder can be used in lattes, teas, porridge, cookies, cakes, baked goods, and virtually all components of the sweet kitchen. It's good to combine it with other flavor agents to camouflage the taste a bit, unless you care for it.

Properties:

- Has a positive impact on the body's circulation
- Contributes to maintaining memory and reducing difficulty concentrating

- Can reduce inflammatory conditions in the body
- An aid in stimulating the production and growth of nerve cells

Hallmarks: Blood thinning and stimulating.

GINSENG

Flavor: Bitter and earthy with a touch of sweetness.

Use: Ginseng is best used in herbal teas, lattes, or soups. It is an excellent alternative to caffeine if you need energy.

Properties:

- Possible support for creating clarity and finding energy or calm when needed
- Can reduce inflammatory conditions
- Has a positive impact on your mental and physical performance
- Good for fatigue and stress

Hallmarks: Stimulates energy.

GOJI BERRIES

Flavor: Sweet and slightly sour.

Use: The texture of goji berries is somewhat reminiscent of raisins, and they can be used in granola, sprinkled over porridge and cakes, or just as a snack.

Properties:

- Loaded with antioxidants, trace minerals, essential amino acids, vitamin C, and beta-carotene
- May have an immune-boosting effect
- Vitalizing properties

Hallmarks: Vitalizing and immune boosting.

GOTU KOLA

Flavor: Bitter.

Use: Gotu kola can be used in everything from desserts, snacks, and tea, to sprinkling on breakfast food or smoothies.

Properties:

- Contributes to calming the nervous system and quieting racing thoughts
- Can stimulate circulation and fight restlessness in the legs
- Has a positive influence on the formation of skin, hair, and nails
- A possible support for wound healing and regeneration

Hallmarks: Nerve-strengthening and regenerating.

HIBISCUS

Flavor: Sour and slightly cranberry-like.

Use: Hibiscus is much more than just a beautiful flower. In addition to tasting delicious in tea, it is also excellent in syrups, desserts, cakes, and other sweets.

Properties:

- Rich in antioxidants
- Can relieve cold symptoms
- Possible support for inhibiting fungi and bacteria in the urinary tract
- Has antibacterial and anti-inflammatory properties
- Supports a healthy cholesterol balance

Hallmarks: Supportive and antibacterial.

LAVENDER

Flavor: Perfumed and slightly bitter.

Use: Lavender can be used in diverse vegetable dishes, tea, and in the sweet kitchen. Lavender sugar and lavender honey are especially worth trying.

Properties:

- Has a positive effect on digestion and bloating
- Can act relaxing on tense muscles
- A help to calm both mind and body
- Support for relieving headaches
- Has healing properties on impure skin, sun damage, and rashes
- Can inhibit bacteria, fungal growth, and parasites

Hallmarks: Balancing and stabilizing.

LEMONGRASS

Flavor: Lemony with a floral touch.

Uses: This thick, fresh stalk is especially known for its characteristic flavor in Asian soups and curry dishes, where it helps balance the rich flavor of coconut milk with its lightness.

Properties:

- Can have an antipyretic effect
- Has antibacterial properties and acts fungicidal
- Rich in antioxidants
- Can contribute to a restful night's sleep
- Good for nervousness and stress
- Supports a natural regulation of the appetite

Hallmarks: Refreshing and antibacterial.

LEMON BALM (HEART'S DELIGHT)

Flavor: Fresh, mild, and acidic.

Use: Lemon balm is good in tea, salads, homemade ice cream, and as a garnish on cakes and other desserts. You can also freshen up dressings and seasoned oil with lemon balm.

Properties:

- Possible support for heart palpitations, excessive thinking, and sleep problems
- Can have a positive impact on colds and flu-like symptoms
- Good for nausea and restlessness in the body
- Can lower fever heat and act as a mild diaphoretic

Hallmarks: Calming and antinauseant.

LICORICE

Flavor: Sweet, slightly spicy, and with a slightly bitter undertone.

Use: Licorice root, and especially the flavor of licorice, is associated most with candy, cakes, and desserts, but the characteristic flavor is also an interesting flavoring agent in tea, vegetable dishes, and bread. It is easiest to use licorice root powder in the home kitchen.

Properties:

- Contributes to lowering the body's cortisol levels
- Has a positive effect on balancing estrogen levels through the woman's cycle
- Good for stress and PMS symptoms
- A possible support for calming the digestive system
- A help with reducing inflammation in the intestinal tract
- Helps stabilize blood sugar and can act to curb sugar cravings
- Can act as an expectorant and cough suppressant

Hallmarks: Calming and pain-relieving.

LINDEN FLOWER

Flavor: Sweet and mild herbal flavor.

Use: Linden flowers can be used in the same way as you would use chamomile, that is, in teas and lattes, as well as in the sweet kitchen.

Properties:

- A help to calm the circulatory and nervous system and therefore good for insomnia and nighttime restlessness
- Can act as a diuretic and remedy fluid retention in the body
- Good for strengthening the body through fever, cold, and flu

Hallmarks: Calming and diuretic.

LION'S MANE MUSHROOM

Flavor: Delicate, umami, and meaty.

Use: Lion's mane can be used across the kitchen in both soups and stews, smoothies, hot drinks, and sweet truffles.

Properties:

- Has a positive effect on the body's immune system
- Can remedy discomfort during menopause
- Good in connection with stomach ulcers and intestinal inflammation
- Helps with mental clarity
- Supports healthy digestion

Hallmarks: Boosts concentration and memory.

LUCUMA

Flavor: Sweet/tart, creamy, and caramel-like.

Use: Lucuma is used in the sweet kitchen primarily for ice cream, cakes, desserts, porridge, and hot drinks, where it can lift the flavor experience and is used instead of sugar. Can be eaten both fresh and in powder form, with the latter being the most commonly used.

Properties:

- Contains fiber and can help against a sluggish stomach
- Filled with antioxidants
- Can have a blood-sugar stabilizing effect

Hallmarks: Blood sugar stabilizing and rich fiber.

MAITAKE MUSHROOM

Flavor: Rich, slightly sweet, and meaty.

Uses: Maitake mushroom is often used in hot and cold drinks and also works well in baked goods.

Properties:

- Can hinder increases in blood sugar levels
- Contributes to inhibiting weight gain and improving fat metabolism
- Is rich in antioxidants
- Can be a good supplement for managing PCOS

Hallmarks: Blood-sugar stabilizing and cell strengthening.

MATCHA

Flavor: Green and grassy.

Use: If you are a coffee drinker, this powder can be a formidable substitute, since it has an invigorating effect, but in a milder way than coffee. Be aware that quality and flavor go hand in hand. Therefore, look for a quality where the powder is completely light green and not yellowish or brownish. Can also be used in cakes, desserts, porridge, and truffles.

Properties:

- Bursting with antioxidants
- Has anti-inflammatory and cleansing properties
- Contributes to increasing energy levels and promoting focus and concentration
- Can be naturally cleansing

Hallmarks: Energy-stimulating and anti-inflammatory.

MILK THISTLE

Flavor: Mild and bitter.

Use: Milk thistle is good primarily in herbal teas and infusions.

Properties:
- Supports the liver's detoxifying function
- Can have a cholesterol-lowering effect
- A possible support for easing estrogen dominance
- Can help lower blood sugar levels

Hallmarks: Liver detoxifying and cleansing.

MINT

Flavor: Spicy and sweet with a citrus aroma.

Use: Mint is a wonderful flavoring agent—not only in a pitcher of water and drinks, but also in salads, baked goods, and desserts.

Properties:
- Can promote digestion and calm the stomach
- Has a positive effect on bad breath
- Can act as an antispasmodic and muscle relaxant
- Possible support for increasing the secretion of stomach acid and relieving nausea
- Has antiviral properties with respiratory diseases
- Helps to stimulate liver function and increase the secretion of bile
- Can relieve cold symptoms
- Supports healthy blood circulation

Hallmarks: Stimulates digestion and relief.

MOUNTAIN CELERY (LOVAGE)

Flavor: Strong and aromatic flavor, slightly reminiscent of celery.

Use: Mountain celery tastes good in soups and stews but can be dominant, so be careful about the amount used. You can also cook a few stalks together with potatoes to give them a delicious flavor.

Properties:
- Can act as a diuretic
- Has anti-inflammatory properties
- Helps soothe skin problems and cramps
- Has previously been perceived as an effective potency agent
- Supports stimulation of milk production in nursing mothers

Hallmarks: Diuretic and aphrodisiac.

MULBERRY

Flavor: Sweet and caramel-like.

Use: The sun-dried bright berries with their sweet caramel flavor are delicious in porridge, bars, granola, or simply as a snack.

Properties:
- Plays a positive role in the immune system
- Can stabilize blood sugar levels
- Supports the body's own cleansing processes
- Packed with antioxidants

Hallmarks: Strengthens immunity and stabilizes blood sugar

MUSTARD SEED

Flavor: Warm, sweet, and slightly biting.

Use: Crushed, whole, and in powder form, mustard seeds can be used in everything from vegetable and rice dishes, to soups, vinegars, and sandwiches.

Properties:

- Contributes to stimulating the appetite
- Possible support for the prevention of indigestion and flatulence
- Supports the excretion of waste products in the body
- Has a warming effect on the body and can help relieve muscle pain and promote blood circulation
- May lower blood pressure

Hallmarks: Digestion regulating, detoxifying, and warming.

NUTMEG

Flavor: Aromatic.

Use: Nutmeg gives delicious depth and a rounding out to sauces, pâtés, and stuffing. Baked goods and cakes can also be spiced up with a dash of grated nutmeg.

Properties:

- Can have a calming effect on menstrual and abdominal pain
- Can help indigestion, nausea, and vomiting
- Can help support the nervous system with fatigue and exhaustion

Hallmarks: Calming and relieving.

OAT STRAW

Flavor: Mildly of oat.

Use: Oat straw often is used dried in tea and tinctures, where it lends an oat flavor. Can also be used in vegetable dishes and stews.

Properties:

- Can uplift a depressed mind
- An aid in restoring the nervous system
- Contributes to calming digestion
- Is mineral-rich and can strengthen skin, hair, and nails
- Grants a more restful sleep and can help with insomnia

Hallmarks: Restorative and calming.

OREGANO

Flavor: Strong, slightly peppery, and bitter.

Use: Oregano is used in sauces, vinaigrettes, stews and simmering dishes, salads, and, of course, on pizza. A must-have in every spice cabinet, fresh, dried, and as oil.

Properties:

- Can have an antibacterial effect
- Helps to counteract osteoporosis
- Good for relieving headaches and colds
- Can remedy flatulence and promote digestion
- Has strong antioxidant properties

Hallmarks: Antibacterial and immune boosting.

PAPRIKA

Flavor: Smoky or sweet.

Use: The red spice can be used in virtually all dishes, like stews, sauces, and toppings, to give a bit of edge and heat. However, not in the same way as chili.

Properties:

- Is rich in vitamin C and can be immune boosting
- Has anti-inflammatory properties
- Contributes to stimulating digestion and fat burning
- Can relieve cold-like symptoms, such as a runny nose and sore throat

Hallmarks: Immune-boosting and digestion supporting.

PARSLEY

Flavor: Slightly bitter and mildly peppery.

Use: This well-known green sprig can be used in a multitude of salads and vegetable dishes, as well as in sauces, dressings, and pesto. Curly parsley is wilder and more aromatic, while flat-leaf parsley is sweeter and mild.

Properties:

- Contributes to promoting digestion and can act as an appetite regulator
- Good for painful menstrual cramps
- Can act as a diuretic and is good against urinary tract infections, fluid retention, and urinary stones
- Contributes to remedy bad breath
- Can have a balancing and regulating effect on the hormonal system

Hallmarks: Digestive promoting and diuretic.

PASSIONFLOWER

Flavor: Faintly fruity and floral.

Use: The curled flower can be used in delicious drinks, hot teas, and in different sweets.

Properties:

- Can calm an uneasy mind and act as a stress reliever
- Has a positive influence on the quality of sleep
- Possible support for counteracting restlessness
- A help with stimulating a feeling of well-being
- Can be antibacterial toward infections

Hallmarks: Calming and nerve regulating.

PEPPER

Flavor: The green is fresh and herbal, the black is hot and aromatic, and the white is warm.

Use: The small stone fruits or peppercorns, as we most commonly know them, are used before, during, and after cooking, in all types of food, and where you just want an extra little kick. If you haven't tried it, pepper is also delicious in desserts and fresh fruit dishes.

Properties:

- Can act as a natural pain reliever
- Contributes to the stimulation of digestion and fat burning
- Supports the flow of heat in the body
- Can act as an expectorant

Hallmarks: Digestive stimulant and warming.

PEPPERMINT

Flavor: Sweet and fresh.

Use: Peppermint is good in warm tea, sweet dishes, and desserts, but is also an interesting feature in savory dishes, where it gives a cooler and slightly peppery flavor.

Properties:

- Helps freshen breath
- Can have a calming effect on the gut with digestive problems and bloating
- Possible support in alleviating cold and flu symptoms
- Can be used for tension headaches or neck stiffness
- Contributes to repressing nausea and can therefore be effective against motion sickness
- Supports appetite stimulation
- Can have a calming effect on the body and mind with insomnia and tension
- A helping hand with relieving sore throats and gingivitis

Hallmarks: Stimulating and soothing.

RASPBERRY (LEAVES)

Flavor: Sour and sweet.

Use: Raspberries are known and loved by many and can be used in a myriad of ways, from jam, juice, and smoothies, to filling for cakes, tarts, and salads. The leaves are good in tea and infusions.

Properties:

- Can ease menstrual cramps
- Supports the balancing of the menstrual cycle
- An aid for softening tendons and ligaments in the birth canal
- Can act as a diaphoretic and reduce heat from fever
- Good for digestion

Hallmarks: Antispasmodic.

REISHI MUSHROOM

Flavor: Bitter.

Use: Reishi mushroom is often used in tea and warm lattes as well as in soups, porridge, smoothies, or other cakes and desserts. It is especially good to consume in the evening.

Properties:

- Can have an invigorating and calming effect on the nervous system
- Has anti-inflammatory and antibacterial properties
- Has a positive effect on respiratory disorders such as hay fever, asthma, pneumonia, and other infections
- Helps to improve the body's blood circulation
- Has a positive influence on the regulation of blood sugar
- A helping hand to strengthen the liver and support detoxification

Hallmarks: Balancing, calming and energizing.

RHODIOLA

Flavor: Bittersweet.

Use: Rhodiola can be mixed into cold drinks like juice and smoothies or enjoyed in hot drinks like herbal tea and latte.

Properties:

- A helping hand to increase mental and physical energy levels
- Can reduce stress and anxiety
- Has a positive influence on stabilizing blood sugar levels

- Can have a calming and mood enhancing effect

Hallmarks: Blood sugar stabilizing and focusing.

ROSE HIPS

Flavor: Sweet-and-sour fruity and floral flavor.

Use: Make compotes and marmalade, use the berry in baked goods and cakes, or sprinkle dried rose hips over your breakfast. The peels are also delicious to use in tea.

Properties:
- Rich nutritional and antioxidant profile
- Can have an anti-inflammatory effect
- Is rich in vitamin C and can therefore support the immune system
- Helps maintain mobility in stiff muscles and joints

Hallmarks: Immune-supporting and anti-inflammatory.

ROSE PETALS

Flavor: Perfumed.

Use: Rose petals can be used in numerous ways in the kitchen and are frequently used in Middle Eastern dishes. They can provide a perfumed and floral flavor element to bread, cakes, and other desserts.

Properties:
- Supports the balancing of the menstrual cycle
- Helps promote radiant, healthy skin
- Has anti-inflammatory and antioxidant properties

Hallmarks: Balancing and calming.

ROSEMARY

Flavor: Robust, slightly bitter, and perfumed.

Use: Rosemary needs heat and is fantastic with baked and roasted vegetables, on pizza, and in stews, soups, sauces, and bread. A refined element in desserts, drinks, and sweets.

Properties:
- Is rich in antioxidants
- Can have a stimulating effect on the production of bile and gastric juices
- Helps promote the body's blood flow
- Can have a soothing effect on muscle and nerve pain
- A helping hand to strengthen memory, sharpen concentration, and ease headaches
- Good against dandruff, lice, and hair loss

Hallmarks: Antioxidant and stimulating.

SAGE

Flavor: Strong, spicy, and lightly perfumed.

Use: Sage is good in dressings, sauces, stews, pot roasts, soups, and fatty foods. Try frying the leaves until they are crispy and use them as a delicious garnish on your dish.

Properties:
- Has a positive effect on inflammation symptoms and fungal diseases, especially in the throat, mouth, and skin
- Can relieve menstrual cramps
- Has diuretic properties and can help to cleanse the body of waste

- Helps to stimulate blood circulation and the nervous system, which can have a beneficial effect on memory and concentration
- Can act as an antiperspirant and relieve discomfort from menopause

Hallmarks: Antiperspirant, antifungal, and soothing.

SEA BUCKTHORN

Flavor: Fresh and sour.

Use: Sea buckthorn can be used in virtually everything, but the berries are wonderful to use in the dessert kitchen, where their sourness complements sweet and rich foods well.

Properties:

- Contains serotonin—the signal substance that creates the feeling of happiness
- Loads of vitamins and antioxidants
- May have a strengthening effect on mucous membranes
- Rich in vitamin C

Hallmarks: Strong antioxidant and mucosa strengthening.

SHIITAKE MUSHROOM

Flavor: Salty, umami, and meaty.

Use: Shiitake powder is delicious in tea, coffee, and soups, but dried or regular mushrooms can also be added to cooking in a myriad of dishes.

Properties:

- Is a powerful antioxidant
- Contains a wealth of vitamins and minerals

- Contributes to maintaining healthy blood pressure and can improve blood circulation
- Can sharpen the ability to concentrate and improve performance
- Helps increase energy levels

Hallmarks: Energizing, anti-inflammatory, and immune boosting.

STAR ANISE

Flavor: Warm, spicy, licorice-like aroma.

Use: These beautiful little stars are used a lot in Chinese cooking, among other things in soups and marinades. Also try them in tea and tinctures, where they provide a delicious flavor.

Properties:

- Can be an expectorant and is therefore a good remedy for cold-like symptoms
- Assists in strengthening the immune system
- Rich in vitamin C and can therefore have an antibacterial effect

Hallmarks: Expectorant and immune boosting.

STINGING NETTLE

Flavor: Mild and spicy.

Use: Stinging nettle is a genuinely universal herb that is suitable for soups, smoothies, juice, pesto, and bread. Preferably use the fresh shoots, as they taste best.

Properties:

- Helps to balance sex hormones
- Can stimulate milk production during breastfeeding

- Has a positive impact on the immune system
- Good for eczema and sore joints
- Rich in iron
- Strengthens skin, hair, and nails
- May act as a diuretic and reduce fluid retention

Hallmarks: Skin cleansing and diuretic.

SPIRULINA

Flavor: Light taste of the sea.
Use: The beautiful blue-green algae is breathtaking in itself, but also gives a nice color and a shot of concentrated nutrition to smoothies, juices, and other drinks, as well as baked goods and truffles.
Properties:

- Has cleansing properties
- Helps to strengthen the heart, bones, and teeth
- Possible support for a normal blood sugar
- Can strengthen the immune system due to the high content of antioxidants
- Has antibacterial properties and can act as an anti-inflammatory
- Supports the body's regeneration and helps promote wound healing

Hallmarks: Cleansing and strengthening.

TARRAGON

Flavor: Slightly spicy, intense, and with notes of licorice.
Use: Tarragon is one of the signature herbs in French cuisine. This herb can cut through rich dishes like a béarnaise sauce and gives a nice edge to creamy dishes.

Properties:

- Can be soothing for toothaches or infections in the mouth, along with abdominal pain
- Has a positive influence on stabilizing blood sugar
- Has anti-inflammatory and pain-relieving properties
- Rich in iron
- Can promote healthy hair and scalp

Hallmarks: Relieving and vitalizing for skin and hair.

THYME

Flavor: Spicy and slightly bittersweet.
Use: Thyme is a popular herb in Mediterranean and European dishes and is often used with other herbs in everything from drinks and dressings to salads, soups, and stews.
Properties:

- Has antibacterial properties and can be especially good for skin and gum problems
- Contributes to calming the mind and digestive system
- Can have an expectorant effect and can therefore be good against respiratory disorders such as hay fever, asthma, pneumonia, and other infections
- Can increase energy levels while also having a muscle-relaxing effect
- Good for stomach cramps and intestinal infections

Hallmarks: Antibacterial.

TURKEY TAIL

Flavor: Bitter and earthy.

Use: Turkey tail can be used in soups, teas, and lattes, as well as cold drinks like smoothies and cold infusions.

Properties:

- May have an antiviral effect
- Contributes to strengthening and supporting the immune system
- Has a positive effect on liver health

Hallmarks: Immune supporting and liver protective.

TURMERIC

Flavor: Mild and slightly bitter.

Use: Turmeric can be used in all kinds of recipes; everything from stews, soups, and smoothies, to hummus, curry dishes, bread, and baked goods. The root is always good in dishes where you also want to use curry. Ground fresh turmeric is sweeter than dried, and you can use three times as much fresh turmeric as dried in cooking.

Properties:

- Has anti-inflammatory properties
- Is rich in antioxidants that protect the brain
- Good for joint pain
- Provides care for an upset stomach
- May reduce the risk of cardiovascular disease
- Supports brain function and therefore has a positive effect on memory

Hallmarks: Anti-inflammatory and protective.

VALERIAN

Flavor: Slightly earthy.

Use: This plant is primarily used in hot drinks, like lattes and teas, as well as syrups and tinctures.

Properties:

- Plays a positive role for your sleep
- Can be calming and relaxing
- Good for muscle tension
- Helps with nervousness, anxiety, and restlessness
- Can have a relieving effect on menstrual pain and stomach cramps

Hallmarks: Calming and relaxing.

WHEATGRASS

Flavor: Bitter, earthy, and grassy.

Use: Wheatgrass powder can be blended into smoothies or drunk straight (possibly with lemon to neutralize the flavor). Also try the powder in porridge, desserts, and other sweets.

Properties:

- Positive effect on the body's natural cleansing process and ability to reduce accumulated waste products
- Can have a stabilizing and balancing effect, especially on diabetes and other insulin problems
- Contributes to oxygenating and cleansing the blood
- Packed with minerals, enzymes, and vitamins

Hallmarks: Cleansing and blood sugar stabilizing.

WILD GARLIC

Flavor: Sour and grassy.

Use: Wild garlic can be used in the same way as you would use regular garlic in a dish. Try using the leaves in pesto, salad, herb butter, or bread.

Properties:

- Can act as a blood pressure regulator
- Has cleansing properties
- Contributes to strengthening the immune system
- Good for bacteria, viruses, and fungal growth

Hallmarks: Cleansing and strengthening.

YARROW

Flavor: Strongly spicy with bitter notes.

Use: Yarrow is particularly good in salads, teas, vegetable dishes, and dressings. The small white or colorful flowers also nicely decorate cakes and desserts.

Properties:

- May have a fever-reducing effect
- Has antibacterial properties and can help fight infections in the skin, throat, and gums
- Helps in the healing of wounds
- Can have a hemostatic effect and ease menstrual cramps
- Good against impure skin, eczema, and rashes
- Contributes to healthy digestion and can reduce flatulence

Hallmarks: Hemostatic and comforting.

Morning time

*Get the best start to the day. Fill up the body's energy stores with easy,
nourishing, and satisfying meals that provide a shot of important
nutrients so that you're ready to seize the day on busy weekdays. Or
use the weekend to turn the tempo down, the coziness up, and enjoy a
late breakfast table with friends and family. Let the aroma of herbal
infusions spread through the room while the hours-long conversations
become memories for life.*

GOLDEN GRANOLA

Morning time has gold in its mouth, in the form of crisp, golden sprinkles with just the right combination of sweet and spicy. Top off your breakfast smoothie or grab a handful as an afternoon snack. You can always perk up your granola with adaptogens, edible flowers, and superfoods.

FOR 1 LARGE BAKING SHEET

FLAXSEED MIXTURE
3 tablespoons ground flaxseed
7 tablespoons water

FOR TOASTING
¼ cup (½ deciliter) olive oil
1 tablespoon maple syrup
1 teaspoon ground ginger
1 teaspoon ground turmeric
2 teaspoons ground Ceylon cinnamon
1 teaspoon freshly ground Himalayan
  salt
½ teaspoon freshly ground black
  pepper

MAIN INGREDIENTS
½ cup (1 deciliter) sunflower seeds
½ cup (1 deciliter) sesame seeds
½ cup (1 deciliter) Brazil nuts, coarsely
  chopped
¼ cup (½ deciliter) chia seeds
½ cup (1 deciliter) coconut flakes
½ cup (1 deciliter) puffed quinoa
½ cup (1 deciliter) walnuts, coarsely
  chopped

Preheat the oven to 320°F (160°C). Mix the ground flaxseed with water in a small bowl and set aside for about 10 minutes. Pour the olive oil and syrup into a large bowl and add the ginger, turmeric, Ceylon cinnamon, Himalayan salt, and pepper. Fold the flaxseed mixture into the spiced oil, and add the kernels, nuts, and seeds. Mix everything together thoroughly until the ingredients are well moistened, using your hands, if necessary.

Now, spread out the granola evenly on a baking sheet covered with parchment paper. Bake for 20 to 25 minutes, or until the granola is golden. Turn the mixture over during baking so it doesn't burn. Remove the baking sheet from the oven and let the granola cool completely. Store the golden mixture in an airtight jar.

UMAMI BREAKFAST PORRIDGE

with avocado and kale

A green mecca of good raw materials accompanied by a creamy porridge that both warms and weighs down in just the right way, and not least, sends the whole spectrum of flavors into full bloom.

FOR 1 PERSON

MAIN INGREDIENTS

⅔ cup (1½ deciliters) gluten-free rolled oats

3¾ cups (7 deciliters) water

3⅓ cups (6 deciliters) kale, finely chopped

2 eggs

coconut oil

TOPPING

2 tablespoons coconut aminos

1 teaspoon sambal oelek

1 handful fresh mushrooms, sliced

1 green onion, finely chopped

¼ large avocado, sliced

½ tablespoon chili oil

Boil the water and rolled oats in a small saucepan. Let the porridge simmer for 4 to 5 minutes. There will still be a lot of water in the pan, so it won't be as thick as usual, but that's exactly how it should be. Meanwhile, prepare the vegetables and set aside. Add an egg to the saucepan and stir vigorously with a wooden spoon so the yolk is really worked into the porridge. When the egg starts to firm slightly, mix in the finely chopped kale. Push the kale down into the porridge so most of it is submerged. Let the porridge simmer for 2 to 3 minutes, stirring occasionally. The kale will slowly lose volume and mix with the oats.

When the porridge has thickened, add 1 tablespoon coconut aminos, 1 teaspoon sambal oelek, and half of the chopped green onion. Mix well. While the porridge is simmering, heat up a pan, add coconut oil, and sweat the mushrooms until they turn brown. Remove them from the pan, and then crack an egg on the pan. Fry the egg according to preference and mood. The egg can also be flipped and fried on both sides.

Arrange the porridge in a deep bowl and top with the fried egg, sliced avocado, the rest of the green onion, and the last tablespoon of coconut aminos and chili oil.

GREEN SHAKSHUKA CRÊPES

Long, lazy mornings are some of the best. The combination of a good time, morning hair, and delicious crêpes is hard to beat. Good morning. Good weekend.

CRÊPES

¾ cup (2 deciliters) coarse rice flour
2 eggs
¾ cup (2 deciliters) almond milk
½ teaspoon freshly ground
  Himalayan salt
coconut oil, for cooking and on
  parchment paper

FILLING

3½ ounces or 1 (4-ounce) package
  (100 grams) goat feta
4 handfuls fresh spinach, roughly
  chopped
2 tablespoons plant-based or salted
  churned butter, divided into 4 thin
  slices
4 eggs
2 small onions, cut into half rings
2 cloves garlic, finely chopped
6 radishes, sliced
½ squash, grated
½ cup (70 grams) green peas
turmeric, to taste
freshly ground Himalayan salt and
  pepper

TOPPING

¼–½ cup (½–1 deciliter) fresh dill,
  coarsely chopped
1 lemon, juice
coconut bacon (see recipe on page 199)
olive oil

Mix the rice flour, almond milk, eggs, and Himalayan salt in a bowl, blender, or mixer. Let the batter rest for about 10 minutes. Heat up coconut oil in a pan, and when the oil has melted, make the first crêpe. Spread the batter out so the crêpe is thin. Cook the crêpe on both sides over medium heat until golden and cooked through, but still slightly soft. Continue in the same way until the four crêpes are made.

Preheat the oven to 350°F (175°C). Heat a pan and cook the onion, garlic, and squash until the mixture turns golden. Season with the turmeric, Himalayan salt, and pepper. Take the pan off the burner.

Place a piece of parchment paper on a baking sheet and grease with a little coconut oil. Place the crêpes on the parchment paper and spread the crumbled cheese, spinach, radishes, and the onion and squash mixture evenly on each crêpe. Place a slice of butter on top and sprinkle with Himalayan salt and pepper. Add the peas and crack an egg into the center of each of the four crêpes. Fold the edges in toward the center to hold the filling and to form a square. You can use toothpicks or skewers to hold the edges. Place the baking sheet in the oven and bake the crêpe pockets for 10 to 12 minutes or until the eggs are finished cooking.

Take the crêpes out of the oven and top with the dill, olive oil, coconut bacon, lemon juice, and freshly ground Himalayan salt and pepper.

COOKIE CUPS
with chili-lemon marinated strawberries

*Did someone say dessert for breakfast? Yes, why not? These fabulous sweet and tart
cookie cups are packed with lots of good nutrients and have a sinfully delicious flavor.*

COOKIE CUPS
¼ cup (½ deciliter) plant-based
  or churned butter, melted
1 large tablespoon honey
1 teaspoon vanilla powder
1 large ripe banana, mashed
2 cups (5 deciliters) gluten-free
  rolled oats, half of it blended
  into flour
1 teaspoon ground Ceylon
  cinnamon
¼ teaspoon freshly ground
  Himalayan salt
2 tablespoons almond milk,
  optional
coconut oil for molds, melted

MARINATED STRAWBERRIES
1½ cups (250 grams) fresh
  strawberries, quartered
¼–½ cup (½–1 deciliter) honey
1 vanilla bean
1 handful basil leaves, finely
  chopped
½ lemon, juice and grated zest
1 tablespoon fresh chili, finely
  chopped

FILLING AND TOPPING
coconut yogurt
vanilla
fresh mint or lemon balm

Marinating the strawberries can be done the day before.

Preheat the oven to 350°F (175°C). Grease a muffin
pan with coconut oil and set aside. Melt the butter and
honey over a water bath, and blend half of the rolled
oats into flour in a grinder, blender, or food processor.
Mash the banana and mix with melted butter, honey,
and vanilla in a bowl. Add the rolled oats, oat flour,
Ceylon cinnamon, and Himalayan salt to the bowl and
mix well. If the dough crumbles too much, moisten with
1 to 2 tablespoons of the optional almond milk. Divide
the dough evenly between 10 to 12 muffin molds. Press
the dough firmly into the bottom of the mold with your
fingers and distribute it up the sides to form a cup. Be
careful not to make the bottom too thin.

Bake the cups for 20 to 25 minutes, or until the edges
are golden and crisp. Let them cool slightly before
removing the cups from the muffin molds.

Grate the lemon zest, split the vanilla bean lengthwise
and scrape out the seeds. Finely chop the basil leaves.
Melt the honey and mix in the vanilla seeds, lemon juice,
lemon zest, basil, and chili. Let the mixture cool down
slightly. Cut the strawberries into quarters and put them
in a bowl. Pour a layer of honey over the strawberries and
fold the mixture well. Pour into a sanitized jar and let them
macerate for 5 to 8 hours, or preferably until the next day.

Top the cups with coconut yogurt with vanilla folded in,
marinated strawberries, and fresh mint or lemon balm.

The cups can be stored in the refrigerator or freezer.

COLORFUL SMOOTHIES

Make colors pop first thing in the morning with a serving of liquid magic that satisfies, nourishes, and makes you happy in your noggin. Then, both body and mind are ready for whatever lies ahead, and for me, it's the best start to the day.

GUIDE FOR COMPOSITION OF SMOOTHIES

You can add a lot of herbs and superfoods to your smoothies, but I recommend keeping them relatively simple for the sake of the digestive system and flavor. I usually put together a smoothie from the following parts:

Fruit—Berries, mango, kiwi, peaches, melon, bananas, pomegranate, pineapple, grapes, apples, limes, oranges, and pears. The possibilities are endless, and fruit is a great source of beneficial vitamins, minerals, and antioxidants. Both fresh and frozen fruit and berries can be used.

Vegetables—All kinds of cabbage, cucumber, sweet potatoes, spinach, beets, broccoli, peas, edamame beans, and carrots. The vegetables contain a lot of nutrition and provide a good flavor.

Herbal infusions—Herbs like stinging nettle, chamomile, elderflower, lavender, oat straw, and hibiscus are packed with vitamins, minerals, and micronutrients. Make infusions by letting 2 tablespoons (¼ deciliter) of herbs steep in 4¼ cups (1 liter) of water for at least 4 hours, and preferably overnight, so the flavor becomes strong and robust.

Digestion-friendly herbs or fresh herbs in general—Ginger, peppermint, lemon balm, anise, licorice, cinnamon, and cardamom are all herbs that stimulate healthy digestion and can be soothing for any imbalances like cramps, gas, and digestive problems. If you want to experiment more, basil and parsley are also delicious flavor agents in the glass.

Liquid—Water, plant milk, coconut water, and yogurt. Liquid helps adjust consistency and provide flavor.

Fats—Coconut oil, tahini, avocado, nuts, hemp seeds, chia seeds, and nut butter. Fats help the body to absorb some of the vitamins in the vegetables better, stabilize blood sugar, provide a greater feeling of satiety, and make a creamier base.

Sweetener—Dates, honey, agave syrup, and stevia. You can always adjust the sweetness up and down, and sometimes the fruit sugar is plenty, in itself.

PEACH, CHAMOMILE, AND LUCUMA SMOOTHIE

1 large peach
1 large carrot
¾ cup (2 deciliters) chamomile infusion
½ cup (1 deciliter) almond or cashew milk
1 tablespoon coconut oil
1 tablespoon lucuma powder
1 teaspoon ground Ceylon cinnamon
3 dates

Blend all of the ingredients until the smoothie is silky and smooth.

BEET, ELDERBERRY, SEA BUCKTHORN, AND ROSE HIP SMOOTHIE

¾ cup (2 deciliters) diced beets, preferably frozen
1 large carrot
¾ cup (2 deciliters) mixed berries, frozen
1¼ cups (3 deciliters) elderflower infusion
½ cup (1 deciliter) almond or cashew milk
1 tablespoon coconut oil
¾–1¼ inches (2–3 centimeters) fresh ginger
4 dates
1 tablespoon hemp seeds
1 tablespoon sea buckthorn, fresh or frozen
1 tablespoon rose hip powder

Peel and dice the beets if you're using raw ones. Blend all of the ingredients until the smoothie is silky and smooth.

MINT, STINGING NETTLE, AND SPIRULINA SMOOTHIE

2 large handfuls kale
¾ cup (2 deciliters) mango, frozen
1¼ cups (3 deciliters) nettle infusion
½ cup (1 deciliter almond) or cashew milk
1 tablespoon coconut oil
1 handful fresh mint
3 dates
1 tablespoon spirulina powder
lemon juice, freshly squeezed and to taste

Blend all of the ingredients until the smoothie is silky and smooth. Top with fresh mint leaves.

Here, you have three suggestions for tasty, colorful smoothies packed with nutrients, but the possibilities are endless, and you can put together a blend as you wish, according to your desire, mood, and taste.

Even though I'm not the first one at home to get out of bed, morning time is one of my absolute favorite times of the day. And the best ones are those where morning can stretch for as long as I want. Without me having to achieve anything—other than snuggling and taking care of my little family and spending a little extra time making a delicious breakfast. But between us, it's not every day that I garnish and decorate my breakfast, and these muffins are just as good without flowers and frills as they are completely au naturel, right out of your hand.

HEARTY BREAKFAST MUFFINS

BREAKFAST MUFFINS

¾ cup + 1 tablespoon + 1 teaspoon (100 grams) gluten-free oat flour

⅜ cup + 2 teaspoons (75 grams) teff flour

1¼ cups (230 grams) cooked butterbeans, rinsed

¾ cup (100 grams) Medjool dates, pitted

1¾ cups (4 deciliters) almond milk

¾ cup (2 deciliters) pure cacao powder

2 teaspoons baking powder

2 tablespoons psyllium husks

1 teaspoon vanilla powder

1 tablespoon lucuma powder

1 tablespoon astragalus powder

1 tablespoon chaga powder

¾ cup (2 deciliters) walnuts, coarsely chopped

¾ cup (2 deciliters) coconut, grated and toasted

½ cup (1 deciliter) collagen powder

½ cup (1 deciliter) chocolate protein powder

1 teaspoon salt

2–3 ripe bananas

TOPPING

chilled coconut cream, whipped

vanilla powder

fresh berries

edible flowers or herbs (wood sorrel, lemon balm, calendula, etc.)

Preheat the oven to 350°F (175°C). Mix all of the dry ingredients except the toasted grated coconut and walnuts in a bowl. Add the mixture to a food processor along with the butterbeans, dates, bananas, and plant milk, and blend into a smooth batter. Fold the toasted grated coconut and walnuts into the batter and divide the mixture among 16 muffin molds.

Bake the muffins for 20 to 25 minutes and let them cool before decorating. They can be frozen and thawed without topping.

Whip the coconut cream (the fatty part from the can) with an electric whisk. For extra volume, you can put the cream in the fridge after whipping the first time, and then whip it again after half an hour. Flavor with a little vanilla powder. Top the muffins with whipped coconut cream, edible flowers, and berries before serving.

BREAKFAST SLICE

Could a luscious morning snack that satisfies, nourishes, and gives you energy to face the joys and challenges of the day tempt you? Grab some finger food on your way out the door or gather the family and share a plate this weekend.

FOR ABOUT 4–6 PEOPLE

EGG BATTER

1¼ cup (230 grams) cooked green lentils

8 eggs

2 large handfuls fresh spinach leaves

2 carrots, grated

1 squash, grated

½ cup (130 grams) goat feta, crumbled

2 large handfuls fresh parsley, coarsely chopped

2 teaspoons freshly ground Himalayan salt

freshly ground pepper

TOPPING

goat cheese or goat feta, crumbled

fresh cherry tomatoes, halved

fresh mint leaves, coarsely chopped

Cook the lentils according to the instructions on the package and drain. Preheat the oven to 400°F (200°C). Whisk the eggs and fold the lentils, spinach, carrots, squash, goat feta, parsley, Himalayan salt, and pepper into the egg batter. Place a piece of parchment paper in an oven safe dish and pour the egg batter into it. Bake the egg batter in the oven for about 45 minutes to 1 hour, or a little longer, until the egg batter is set and the top is golden.

Top with fresh mint, fresh cherry tomatoes, and crumbled goat feta.

NICE CREAM
with sea buckthorn

Who wouldn't want to eat dessert for breakfast? In 5 minutes, you can turn boring, overripe, frozen bananas into the most delicious, creamy, soft ice cream that can be varied to infinity. This recipe is fresh, light, and bursting with vitamin C.

ABOUT 2 PEOPLE

NICE CREAM
2 cups (400 grams) bananas,
  frozen and in small pieces
½ cup (1 deciliter) sea
  buckthorn, frozen
2 handfuls fresh mint
2 tablespoons lucuma powder
2 scoops collagen powder
almond milk, to desired
  consistency

TOPPING
berries and/or fruit
coconut flakes
various superfoods, like açai,
  bee pollen, spirulina, or goji
  berries, to top

Blend all of the ingredients in a food processor to make a quick version of soft ice cream. Adjust the consistency along the way with almond milk. Top with fruit and/or berries, coconut flakes, and various superfoods of choice.

Sometimes, it's the simplest things that spark the greatest excitement. There's nothing like sinking your teeth into a piece of fresh-baked goods, where the crust is crispy and crunches between your teeth, while the springy, moist, and airy crumb invites you to an extra layer of soft butter. Presence, time, and patience can provide great flavor, while kneading with your hands and rolling out dough on the kitchen table is almost meditative. So remember to unplug and grab an extra bite . . . just because.

Soft and crisp breads

SUPERFOOD MUFFINS

Small green energy bombs bursting with great nutrients to start the morning, elevate the afternoon, or save a day on the go.

MUFFINS
1⅓ cups (150 grams) quinoa flour
1¼ cups (150 grams) gluten-free oat flour
3⅓ cups packed (100 grams) fresh spinach
5 eggs
2 teaspoons freshly ground Himalayan salt
⅓ cup (50 grams) almonds
1 tablespoon spirulina powder
1 tablespoon rose hip powder
1 tablespoon lucuma powder
1 teaspoon baking powder
1 squash, grated
2 tablespoons walnut oil
Plant-based butter or oil to grease the muffin pan, optional

TOPPING
½ cup (1 deciliter) pistachios, chopped
pistachio butter, to taste

Prepare the vegetables and blend all ingredients—except walnut oil, pistachios, and squash—in a food processor. Then fold in the walnut oil and grated squash. Divide the batter among the muffin pan and top with pistachio butter and chopped pistachios.

Bake these green muffins for 15 to 20 minutes at 400°F (200 °C). Remove them from the muffin pan and let them cool on a wire rack before enjoying.

CHEESE SCONES
with sautéed red onions

When the landscape changes color and the autumn storms rage, there is nothing cozier than crawling under a blanket. Let the quiet calm of Sunday sink in and indulge in something warm and flavorful.

INGREDIENTS

1 cup (2½ deciliters) cassava flour

1 cup (2½ deciliters) gluten-free oat flour

1 teaspoon baking powder

¼ teaspoon baking soda

⅔ cup (1½ deciliters) plant-based or regular crème fraîche

1 egg

2 teaspoons honey

1⅛ cups (125 grams) plant-based or regular cheddar cheese, grated

8 tablespoons plant-based or churned butter

1–2 teaspoons caraway seeds

1 large red onion, cut in half rings

1 teaspoon freshly ground Himalayan salt

½ teaspoon freshly ground pepper

coconut oil

1 handful cassava flour or gluten-free oat flour for rolling out

flake salt to top

Take the butter out of the refrigerator and let it soften. Heat a pan and toast the caraway seeds for a minute. They shouldn't burn or scorch. Set them aside. Sauté the onions in coconut oil until they're soft and translucent.

Preheat the oven to 400°F (200°C) and prepare a baking sheet with parchment paper. While the oven is preheating, mix the flour, baking soda, baking powder, caraway seeds, and Himalayan salt in a bowl. Whisk the eggs, crème fraîche, and honey together in another bowl.

Distribute the pats of butter in the bowl with the dry ingredients and work the dough together well with your fingers. Pour in the liquid ingredients (eggs, crème fraîche, and honey) and knead the dough well. Finally, fold the sautéed red onions and grated cheddar into the dough.

Spread some flour on the kitchen counter and roll out the dough into a thick pancake. It should be about ¾ to 1¼ inches (2 to 3 centimeters) thick. Cut the dough into eight triangles and place them on the baking sheet lined with parchment paper. Brush the triangles with a little crème fraîche and sprinkle some flake salt over them before putting them in the oven. Bake them for 15 to 20 minutes, until the top is golden and the bottom is a little darker. Let them cool for 10 to 15 minutes before serving.

CRISPBREAD
with stinging nettle and wild garlic

Square, practical, good. Crispy bites for little hands hungry for a snack, or a big appetite at the dinner table. Top them, butter them, or eat them as they are.

INGREDIENTS
¾ cup (2 deciliters) sunflower kernels

⅔ cup (1½ deciliters) sesame seeds

½ cup (1 deciliter) pumpkin seeds

½ cup (1 deciliter) flaxseed

1 teaspoon freshly ground Himalayan salt

¾ cup (2 deciliters) chufa flour

⅔ cup (1½ deciliters) gluten-free oat flour

1 teaspoon baking powder

½ cup (1 deciliter) olive oil

¾ cup (2 deciliters) water

¼ cup (½ deciliter) dried stinging nettle

¼ cup (½ deciliter) wild garlic

Start by turning on the oven at 350°F (175°C). Mix all of the ingredients together in a large bowl and use your hands to knead the dough together well, if necessary. Divide the dough in half and place one batch on a piece of parchment paper. Place another piece of parchment paper on top, grab a rolling pin, and roll out the dough as thinly as possible. The thinner the dough is rolled out, the crispier the crispbread will be. Carefully lift off the top piece of parchment paper. With a pizza wheel or a sharp knife, cut pieces of the dough into the desired shape. Follow the same procedure for the second batch of dough.

Then place the parchment paper with the dough on a baking sheet and bake the crispbread for about 15 to 20 minutes. Keep an eye on it along the way, since it should be golden but not browned.

When the crispbread looks ready, put it on a baking rack to cool. Store it in an airtight glass jar or other container if they don't manage to get eaten before.

There's almost no limit to what the crispbread can be topped with, so experiment with your favorite toppings.

TWISTED HERB BREAD

with real goat cheese

For some, love is an expensive, shiny watch. For others, it's moist, freshly baked bread with a crispy crust. If your love language is also food, you'll love this recipe that combines the weight of the crumb with a salty sweetness from the goat cheese and the bitter uplift from the herbs.

MAIN INGREDIENTS
2 cups (450 milliliters) water

3 tablespoons psyllium husks

¾ cup + 1 tablespoon + 1 teaspoon (100 grams) buckwheat flour

⅝ cup (100 grams) rice flour

¾ cup + 1 tablespoon + 1 teaspoon (100 grams) gluten-free oat flour

⅓ cup (40 grams) tapioca flour

1 teaspoon baking powder

1 teaspoon baking soda

1 teaspoon freshly ground Himalayan salt

FILLING
2 tablespoons (25 grams) plant-based or churned butter, melted

2¼ cups (250 grams) ripe goat cheese, grated

1 large handful parsley, chopped

1 large bunch chives, chopped

1 handful thyme sprigs, picked

1 sprig rosemary, picked and chopped

1 handful oregano sprigs, picked

1 large handful basil, chopped

Start by mixing the psyllium husks and water in a bowl. Whisk for about 5 minutes, or until it starts to form a thick jelly. Then set the bowl aside. In another bowl, add the flour, baking powder, baking soda, and Himalayan salt. Mix everything together well, and fold in the psyllium husk jelly. Knead the dough well for about 5 to 10 minutes with either an electric whisk, a mixer, or just by hand.

Roll out the dough into a square so it roughly fits a piece of parchment paper. Brush the surface with melted butter and sprinkle with the grated real goat cheese. Toss all the chopped herbs together in a bowl so they're mixed well and distribute them over the dough as the next layer over the cheese.

Roll the dough into a roulade on the short side. Then cut it down the middle, lengthwise, but leave one end together so the cut doesn't split the dough in half, but simply makes two "arms" of dough. Twist the two ends around each other, alternating over and under, letting the openings in the dough face upward. Finish by pressing the ends together well so the bread is seamed.

Let the bread rise under a cloth while the oven preheats to 350°F (175°C). Bake the bread for about 50 to 60 minutes.

Serve it with a delicious salad or as a side dish for a warm summer barbecue evening.

DANISH PASTRY BOWS (FRØSNAPPERSLØJFER)
with homemade spiced cheese

In this recipe, the puff pastry is replaced with a gluten-free yeast dough that gives more bite and is more filling.

YEAST DOUGH
⅝ cup (45 grams) tapioca flour
¾ cup + 1½ teaspoons (130 grams) rice flour
¼ cup (45 grams) whole-grain rice flour
½ cup + 1 tablespoon + 1 teaspoon (75 grams) cornstarch
1 tablespoon (10 grams) xanthan gum
1½ teaspoons dry yeast
2½ tablespoons (45 grams) maple syrup
1 teaspoon freshly ground Himalayan salt
½ teaspoon ground cilantro
3 tablespoons (45 grams) plant-based or churned butter, melted
⅔ cup (1½ deciliters) lukewarm water
3 eggs
1 handful tapioca flour, whole-grain rice flour, or regular rice flour, for rolling out
poppy and sesame seeds

FILLING
1–1½ cups (150–200 grams) plant-based or regular, neutral spreadable cheese, depending on how cheesy you want them
2 large handfuls mixed fresh herbs (chives, parsley, dill, thyme, and basil), finely chopped
1 teaspoon garlic powder
lemon juice, freshly squeezed
freshly ground Himalayan salt and pepper

Mix all of the flours together in a large bowl and add the rest of the dry ingredients (cornstarch, xanthan gum, dry yeast, Himalayan salt, and ground cilantro). Fold the melted butter, syrup, 2 of the 3 eggs, and lukewarm water into dough. Knead the dough in a mixer, if you have one. Alternatively, an electric whisk can be used. Start at low speed, then increase to full speed for 5 minutes. Now let the dough rise under plastic wrap for 3 hours.

When the dough has risen, put it in the fridge for an hour or overnight. Sprinkle some flour over the kitchen table and roll out the dough into a square so it takes up the same amount of space as a piece of parchment paper. Mix the chopped herbs with the spreadable cheese and season with garlic powder, lemon juice, Himalayan salt, and pepper. Then, spread the herbed cheese on half of the dough, and fold the other part of the dough over. Lightly press the sides together. Cut the piece of dough in half with a horizontal cut. Cut the dough into ¾-inch × 2¼-inch (2-centimeter × 6-centimeter) short, oblong strips and twist each one into a *frøsnapper*. Place them on a baking sheet lined with parchment paper and plastic wrap and let them proof for a few hours.

Turn on the oven at 355°F (180°C). Beat the last egg and brush the twists while the oven preheats. Sprinkle with the desired amount of poppy and sesame seeds. Bake for 15 to 20 minutes, or until golden.

The frøsnappers taste best warm, crisp, and freshly baked.

BRUSCHETTA

with figs, goat cheese, and sage honey

The fourth meal, the appetizer, the munchies, snacks, pre-dinner. A mini meal that should not only be delicious and inviting, but also should be able to be eaten with one hand, play with different nuances of flavor, and play two or more textures off of each other. There are gradually many demands for the little extra bite, which should be easy to prepare and within reach when a craving strikes or when the stomach starts to growl.

ABOUT 12 PIECES

BRUSCHETTA
1 baguette, in 12 slices
3 large figs, in 12 wedges
6.3-ounce wheel (180 grams)
 ripe goat cheese, sliced
olive oil for brushing
freshly ground Himalayan salt

SAGE HONEY
⅓ cup (¾ deciliter) honey
15–20 fresh sage leaves

Preheat the oven to 400°F (200°C). Heat the honey and sage in a small saucepan and stir constantly for about 10 minutes. Then, take the saucepan off the burner and let it sit to infuse. The honey can be made earlier in the day if you want a stronger flavor.

Cut the baguette into 12 slices and place them on a baking sheet lined with parchment paper. Brush the slices with olive oil and sprinkle a little Himalayan salt over them. Place 1 to 2 slices of goat cheese on each slice of bread, depending on what kind of bread you use, and top with a fig wedge.

Bake the bruschetta for about 8 to 10 minutes, or until the bread is crisp and the goat cheese is golden and slightly melted.

Drizzle some sage honey over before serving, and top with a fresh sage leaf or one from the pan, Himalayan salt, and pepper.

SCOTTISH SHORTBREAD
with rosemary

These little cheese cookies are a fun size and a fantastic alternative to chips. Serve them as they are with a chilled glass of liquid grapes or as part of an informal, finger-greasing tapas dish.

INGREDIENTS

¾ cup (80 grams) chufa flour

½ cup + 1 tablespoon +
1 teaspoon (70 grams) tapioca
flour or gluten-free oat flour

1 cup (100 grams) plant-based
or regular Parmesan cheese,
finely grated

2 tablespoons fresh rosemary,
finely chopped

½ teaspoon freshly ground
Himalayan salt

½ teaspoon freshly ground
pepper

¼ cup + 3 tablespoons (100
grams) plant-based or
churned butter, softened and
at room temperature

various herbs for garnish (sage
leaves, parsley, lavender, and
thyme work well)

Blend all ingredients together in a food processor until the dough comes together. Add a little water, as needed, if the dough seems too dry. Turn the dough out onto the table and knead it with your hands until the dough is soft and without dry flour spots. Roll the dough relatively flat, wrap it in plastic or a piece of reusable parchment paper, and refrigerate for an hour.

Preheat the oven to 350°F (175°C). Roll out the dough to about ¼ inch (½ centimeter) thick between two pieces of parchment paper. If you want to garnish your shortbread, place the herbs between the dough and the top piece of parchment paper with plenty of space in between. Then roll a few extra times to press the herbs lightly into the dough. Cut out small cookies with a cutter that is about 2 inches (5 centimeters) in diameter. Remove the excess dough, roll it out again, and repeat the process until all of the dough is used.

Bake the small shortbreads for 15 to 20 minutes if you want them crisp, and 10 to 15 minutes if you want them a little softer. Let them cool on a wire rack before serving.

You can experiment a lot with these little cookies. For example, try replacing rosemary with thyme or sage, Parmesan cheese with another firm cheese, or garnish with edible flowers, instead.

RUSTIC MUSHROOM AND HERBED CHEESE BAGELS

Bagels take me back to the time when I lived in New York and often had such a breakfast bandit, along with a green juice from a small health cafe around the corner. I got extra cream cheese, obviously, because it's all about balance, right?

ABOUT 8-10 BAGELS

INGREDIENTS

1¾ cups (4 deciliters) water
2 tablespoons psyllium husks
1 cup (100 grams) quinoa flour
⅔ cup (100 grams) whole-grain rice flour
½ cup (1 deciliter) pumpkin seeds
1 teaspoon dry yeast
1 teaspoon freshly ground Himalayan salt
1 tablespoon coconut sugar
1 tablespoon olive oil
1 tablespoon fresh oregano
1 handful fresh basil, finely chopped
1 small handful fresh thyme
¼–½ cup (½–1 deciliter) plant-based or regular cheese, grated
1 egg, for brushing

Whisk water and psyllium husks into a jelly-like substance in a bowl. Then blend in the rest of the ingredients, except the eggs and grated cheese, and refrigerate the dough overnight with a cloth over it.

The next morning, knead the dough lightly. Make 8 to 10 dough sausages to stick together to make a bagel with a hole in the middle. Place them on a baking sheet with parchment paper and let them proof for 10 to 15 minutes. Beat the egg, brush the bagels, and sprinkle the grated cheese over. Bake them in the oven at 400°F (200°C) for about 30 to 40 minutes.

GATHERING

Some of the best and most life-affirming moments occur when we gather across from generations around the dinner table, get our fingers greasy, and throw away table manners for a while. Experience the joy of rubbing elbows with those closest to you, or perhaps someone you hardly know, while narratives unfold and laughter spreads like little pockets of happiness around the body. It is precious moments like these, when people meet and conversations flow, that make dinner into more than just a meal.

If there's anything Italians are known for, it's their magical ability to turn flour, water, and eggs into a multitude of gastronomic delights that many long for and often travel far to taste. Dream of Italy while you wind spaghetti around your fork to the sound of soft violin notes.

SPICY BEAN BALLS IN TOMATO SAUCE

BEAN BALLS
1¾ cups (400 grams) cooked black beans
1¼ cups (3 deciliters) gluten-free rolled oats
2 tablespoons olive oil
1 tablespoon tomato paste
2 teaspoons freshly ground Himalayan salt
3 cloves garlic
1 onion
1 good handful fresh cilantro
2 tablespoons psyllium husks
2 eggs
coconut oil, for sautéing

TOMATO SAUCE
coconut oil
1 large onion, finely chopped
4 cloves garlic, finely chopped
3 cans diced tomatoes
1 apple, finely chopped
1 tablespoon Dijon mustard
1–2 tablespoons tomato paste
2 tablespoons sun-dried tomatoes, finely
  chopped
1 tablespoon coconut sugar
1 teaspoon apple cider vinegar
2 teaspoons fresh rosemary, finely chopped
3 teaspoons liquid basil
freshly ground Himalayan salt

ADDITIONS AND TOPPINGS
pea, lentil, or bean pasta
fresh basil
freshly ground black pepper
yeast flakes

Blend all the ingredients for the bean balls into a smooth dough in a food processor. Make about 20 balls measuring about 1¼ inches (3 centimeters) in diameter. It roughly equals a rounded heaping teaspoon. Sauté them in a pan over medium heat in coconut oil.

Meanwhile, prepare the ingredients for the tomato sauce. Sauté the onion and garlic in a pan with coconut oil until the onions are translucent and tender. Then add the remaining ingredients.

When the balls are almost done, add them to the tomato sauce and let them simmer, covered, for about 10 to 15 minutes. Meanwhile, cook the pasta. If you want your tomato sauce smoother, you can blend it with an immersion blender.

Cook the pea, lentil, or bean pasta according to the package directions.

Serve and top with fresh basil, freshly ground black pepper, and yeast flakes.

These bean balls are similar to meat, but the texture is doughier and is more reminiscent of a dumpling. But they're still delicious.

125

PULLED BBQ JACKFRUIT TACOS

Tacos are Mexican finger food at its finest. The love for Mexican street food is enormous, and the play of colors in the food is a true delight to both the palate and the eyes, so wash your hands well, yawn loudly, and enjoy!

PURPLE CORN PANCAKES
1½ cups (3½ deciliters) purple corn flour

1 cup (2½ deciliters) tapioca flour

1 teaspoon freshly ground Himalayan salt

1 cup (2½ deciliters) boiling water

FILLING
2 cans jackfruit, mashed and separated

½ teaspoon olive oil or coconut oil

4 cloves garlic, finely chopped

1 small onion, finely chopped

1 can diced tomatoes

1 tablespoon tomato paste

2 tablespoons maple syrup

1 teaspoon apple cider vinegar

1 teaspoon tamari or coconut aminos

1 teaspoon Dijon mustard

1 teaspoon freshly ground Himalayan salt

½ teaspoon ground paprika

Start by preparing the batter for the corn pancakes. Pour the corn flour into a medium bowl. Add boiling water, stir, and let it stand for about 10 minutes. Add the tapioca flour and Himalayan salt and mix well. Add more flour, if necessary. Knead the dough for about 5 minutes, and divide it into 10 equal-sized balls. Roll out each ball thinly so it's a maximum of ⅛ to ³⁄₁₆ inch (3 to 5 millimeters). Cook the tortillas on a hot frying pan at high heat for about 3 minutes or until browned on each side. Set them aside on a plate with a cloth over it until the jackfruit filling and additions are ready.

Prepare the ingredients for the filling and drain the jackfruit. Heat up oil in a medium-sized saucepan. Add the garlic and onion and sauté until the onions become tender and translucent. Be sure to stir regularly so the garlic doesn't burn. Add the diced tomatoes, tomato paste, maple syrup, apple cider vinegar, tamari, and mustard to the saucepan. Stir the mixture. Add the Himalayan salt, paprika, cayenne pepper, cumin, chili, ground pepper, and Ceylon cinnamon. Stir. Let the mixture simmer over low to medium heat for 12 to 15 minutes, stirring occasionally. Be careful that the heat isn't too high because the sauce mixture will

¼ teaspoon ground chili
½ teaspoon ground cumin
½ teaspoon cayenne pepper
1 pinch ground Ceylon
  cinnamon
½ teaspoon freshly ground
  pepper

CASHEW CREAM
½ cup (1 deciliter) cashew nuts,
  soaked
water to desired consistency
2 tablespoons lemon juice,
  freshly squeezed
½ clove garlic
fresh cilantro
freshly ground Himalayan salt
  and pepper

ADDITIONS
1 head red cabbage, thinly cut
1 bunch radishes, thinly cut
2 handfuls cherry tomatoes,
  halved
1 bunch green onions, finely
  chopped
1 lime, in wedges
1 handful fresh cilantro,
  coarsely chopped, optional

start to boil and splatter. Mash the jackfruit with the flat side of a knife and add to the sauce.

Let it simmer, covered, for 15 to 20 minutes or until the jackfruit has absorbed some of the sauce.

While the jackfruit absorbs, prepare the cabbage, radishes, tomatoes, green onions, lime, and cilantro. Cook up the tomatoes quickly in a pan with Himalayan salt and pepper and blend the ingredients for the cashew cream. Taste it along the way. Finally, fill the corn pancakes with jackfruit and vegetables and top with cashew cream.

If you have leftover pancakes, you can easily turn them into tortilla chips with just olive oil and Himalayan salt. Brush both sides of your pancakes with oil. Cut them into triangles. Place them on a baking sheet and sprinkle with Himalayan salt. Bake at 400°F (200°C) for 7 to 10 minutes, or until they are golden and crisp.

SWEET POTATO AND ROSEMARY GNOCCHI

Extend the weekend's coziness with these sweet potato gnocchi, which, like pasta, come in countless varieties. The crisp skin forms around a soft interior, and the deep orange bites are accompanied by a browned butter sauce and fresh herbs. Genuine everyday comfort food.

GNOCCHI

2 large sweet potatoes (about 1½ pounds or 700 grams), diced

1¾ cups + 1 teaspoon (250 grams) cassava flour

1½ teaspoons freshly ground Himalayan salt

½ teaspoon onion powder

2 cloves garlic, crushed

½ teaspoon nutmeg, finely grated

½ cup (1 deciliter) yeast flakes

1 teaspoon ground turmeric

1 teaspoon fresh rosemary, finely chopped

1 handful cassava flour, for rolling out

butter or coconut oil, for sautéing

BUTTER SAUCE

2–3 rounded tablespoons plant-based or churned butter

½ onion, halved and in rings

2 cloves garlic, finely chopped

FOR SERVING

3 tablespoons pistachios, coarsely chopped

yeast flakes, or plant-based or regular Parmesan cheese

fresh parsley and sprouts

Peel the sweet potatoes and dice them into medium-sized cubes. Bring water to a boil in a large pot. Add the potatoes, put the lid on the pot, and cook them for about 15 minutes until tender. Drain the water, let the sweet potatoes cool down a bit, and mash them well. Mix the other ingredients for the dough in with the mashed sweet potatoes, and knead the dough with your hands, if necessary. Sprinkle some cassava flour on the kitchen table. Take a lump of dough and roll it out to about a 1½-inch (4-centimeter) wide sausage shape. Cut small slices of the dough of about ½ inch (1½ centimeters), so all the bites are roughly the same size. Place them with one of the large surfaces facing down, take a fork, and lightly press against the dough so fine grooves form on the surface. Continue until all of the dough is rolled out and shaped into small gnocchi bites. Heat up a pan and add coconut oil or butter until the pan is well greased. Turn down to medium heat and fry the small bites for about 5 to 7 minutes on each side or until golden and crisp. Then place them on a piece of paper towel to absorb the fat.

When all of the gnocchi are fried, heat up the butter for the sauce in a saucepan. Sauté the onion and garlic over medium heat until tender and glazed. Meanwhile, chop the pistachios and parsley. Quickly toss the gnocchi in the pan with the butter sauce before serving.

Arrange on plates, drizzle with butter sauce, and top with fresh parsley, sprouts, chopped pistachios, yeast flakes or Parmesan cheese, and freshly ground salt and pepper.

If there are bites left over, they can be stored in an airtight container in the refrigerator for about 3 days once they've cooled down. Subsequently heat them up in a pan or in the oven.

QUESADILLAS
with apples, goat cheese, and chipotle

Crisp on the outside and soft on the inside. This wonderful Mexican food is a hit not only for dinner, but also as a quick lunch or a go-to snack. Genuine comfort food that can be prepared easily and pleases the palate.

FILLING
1 large sweet potato
½ apple, sliced
1 large onion, halved and in rings
¼–⅓ log of goat cheese, sliced
1½–2 tablespoons chipotle in
    adobo sauce
1 tablespoon plant-based or
    churned butter
coconut oil, for frying
2 tortilla pancakes
coconut oil

CREAMY CHIPOTLE SAUCE
2 tablespoons lime juice, freshly
    squeezed
4 tablespoons tahini
2–3 tablespoons chipotles in
    adobo sauce
4 tablespoons olive oil
1 teaspoon ground turmeric
½ cup (1 deciliter) almond milk
1 teaspoon freshly ground
    Himalayan salt

SERVING
fresh herbs (mint, parsley, and/
    or cilantro), coarsely chopped

Preheat the oven to 400°F (200°C). Peel the sweet potato, dice it into medium-sized cubes and bake them in the oven for about 30 to 40 minutes. Keep an eye on them along the way and bake them for a shorter time if they're starting to get dry. They should stay tender and moist. Blend the baked sweet potato cubes in the blender together with the butter and chipotles in adobo. Season with the chipotles in adobo depending on how spicy the mashed potatoes will be. Halve the onion and slice it. While the sweet potatoes are baking, prepare the rest of the ingredients for the filling. Sauté the onion rings in coconut oil in a pan with salt and pepper.

Meanwhile, heat up a pan and spread out the mashed potatoes on a tortilla. Then distribute the fried onion rings, apple slices, and goat cheese over the mashed potatoes. Place another tortilla on top as a lid and lightly press together. Toast the quesadilla in a little coconut oil on both sides until they're golden and crispy.

Blend the ingredients for the chipotle sauce and taste as you go.

Before serving, cut the quesadilla into 6 or 8 triangles and top with creamy chipotle sauce and fresh herbs. Serve with a good salad or make a double portion and eat them alone.

BAKED SWEET POTATOES

with 3 kinds of filling

A cozy little pocket filled and topped with rainbow-colored love. And we all know that a round of baked (sweet) potatoes is undeniably the most fun when they're accompanied by something fresh, crispy, and creamy.

ABOUT 2 PEOPLE

SWEET POTATOES

2 large sweet potatoes

Preheat the oven to 355°F (180°C). Poke holes in the potatoes with a fork and place them on a baking sheet lined with parchment paper. Bake the sweet potatoes for 30 to 60 minutes, or until they're tender. It depends a lot on the size. Meanwhile, make the filling for the potatoes.

Suggestions for 3 different kinds of filling:

SPINACH, POMEGRANATE, AND CRISPY CHICKPEAS

CRISPY CHICKPEAS
1 can cooked chickpeas
1 teaspoon freshly ground
  Himalayan salt
1 tablespoon fresh rosemary,
  finely chopped
freshly ground pepper
olive oil

**SAUTEED SPINACH, ONION,
AND GARLIC**
4 handfuls fresh spinach
2 cloves garlic, finely chopped
1 large onion, diced or in quarter
  rings
freshly ground Himalayan salt
  and pepper
coconut oil, for sautéing

TAHINI DRESSING
2 tablespoons tahini
3 tablespoons water
½ lemon, juice
freshly ground Himalayan salt
  and pepper
½ cup (1 deciliter) pomegranate
  arils, fresh and just cut

Rinse the chickpeas thoroughly and dry them in a clean tea towel or cloth. Toss them well with olive oil in a bowl, then add the fresh rosemary, 1 teaspoon Himalayan salt, and a little pepper to the mixture. Spread the chickpeas out on a baking sheet lined with parchment paper, and toast them in the oven for about 40 minutes until crispy while the potatoes are baking. Turn them once or twice along the way.

Then heat coconut oil in a pan and sauté the onion and finely chopped garlic. When the onions are translucent and tender, add in the spinach. Let it cook until the spinach wilts. Season with Himalayan salt and pepper.

Finally, blend the tahini, 3 tablespoons of water, and lemon juice into a tahini dressing in a food processor. Season with Himalayan salt and pepper.

When the potatoes are done, cut lengthwise down the middle of the potato and break it open slightly. Dig out some of the inside of the potatoes with a fork. Fill the sweet potatoes with the sautéed spinach and top with the tahini dressing, crispy chickpeas, and pomegranate arils.

RED CABBAGE, GOAT CHEESE, AND TOASTED WALNUTS

MIXED FILLING
½ cup (1 deciliter) walnuts
2 handfuls red cabbage, thinly
  cut
½ apple, diced
¼–½ goat cheese log, crumbled
  [author doesn't indicate what
  size cheese log?]

PARSLEY PESTO
2 cups (5 deciliters) fresh
  parsley
¼ cup (30 grams) pine nuts
½ cup (1 deciliter) olive oil
2 tablespoons (10 grams) yeast
  flakes or 1 handful plant-based
  or regular Parmesan cheese
1 clove garlic
freshly ground Himalayan salt
  and pepper

Heat up a dry pan and toast the walnuts until they're golden and crispy. Chop them coarsely. Blend the parsley, pine nuts, Parmesan or yeast flakes, garlic, olive oil, Himalayan salt, and pepper into a smooth and soft pesto.

When the potatoes are done, cut lengthwise down the middle of the potato and break it open slightly. Dig out some of the inside of the potatoes with a fork. Fill the sweet potatoes with the finely chopped red cabbage, and top with the pesto, crumbled goat cheese, diced apples, and toasted walnuts.

SEITAN, CASHEW CREAM, AND CARAMELIZED ONIONS

SAUTEED KALE AND ONION
2 large handfuls kale, coarsely chopped
2 onions, halved and in rings
1 tablespoon dark balsamic vinegar
1 tablespoon coconut sugar
1¼ cloves garlic, finely chopped
freshly ground Himalayan salt and pepper
coconut oil, for sautéing

FRIED SEITAN
¾ cup (100 grams) seitan, sliced
coconut oil, for frying
freshly ground Himalayan salt and pepper

CASHEW CREAM
⅔ cup (1½ deciliters) cashew nuts, soaked
½–⅔ cup (1–1½ deciliters) water
½ lemon, juice
2 tablespoons yeast flakes
3 teaspoons chipotles in adobo sauce
¼–½ clove garlic

FRESH VEGETABLES
½ avocado, sliced
1 handful fresh cilantro, coarsely chopped
½ lime, juice

Blend the soaked cashews, water, lemon juice, yeast flakes, garlic, and chipotles in adobo into a smooth cashew cream. Season with chipotles in adobo, depending on how strong you want it to be. Let it stand and infuse while the rest of the filling is made.

Heat coconut oil in a pan and fry the seitan slices golden and crisp. Remove the slices from the pan and add a little more coconut oil, if necessary.

Sauté the onions over medium heat until they start to take on a little color and turn golden. Next, add the coconut sugar, balsamic vinegar, Himalayan salt, and pepper. Sauté gently around the pan. Let it simmer a bit and taste the onions, if necessary.

When the potatoes are almost ready, heat the coconut oil in a pot or pan. Add the kale and cook until it softens up. Add the garlic, Himalayan salt, and pepper, and continue to cook for a few more minutes. Keep the kale warm until the potatoes are done.

When the potatoes are done, make a cut lengthwise down the middle of the potato and break it open slightly. Dig out some of the inside of the potatoes with a fork and add your toppings. Start with the kale and seitan, then add the caramelized onions, avocado, and cashew cream. Garnish with cilantro. Squeeze a little juice from the ½ lime over the two potatoes to finish.

You can eventually eat the potato filling on the side, folded with a little butter and herbs.

BUTTER-FRIED POINTED CABBAGE

with crispy chickpeas and herb gravy

Pointed cabbage is one of the easiest types of cabbage to work with in the kitchen, because it tastes absolutely excellent stewed, raw, fried, baked, grilled, and steamed. Here, the elliptical, versatile summer cabbage is served butter-fried, with crispy chickpeas, and a green, spring variation of the classic brown gravy.

BUTTER-FRIED POINTED CABBAGE

1 large pointed cabbage
2 tablespoons (30 grams) plant-based or churned butter
freshly ground Himalayan salt and pepper

CRISPY CHICKPEAS

2 cans cooked chickpeas, drained and rinsed
¼ cup (½ deciliter) olive oil
4 tablespoons dried wild garlic
Himalayan salt

HERB GRAVY

2 cups (5 deciliters) water
½ onion, diced
1 handful fresh parsley, finely chopped
3 dried bay leaves
freshly ground pepper
1 small handful thyme, finely chopped
2 teaspoons bouillon
4–5 tablespoons cornstarch

TOPPING

½ lemon, juice
yeast flakes or grated plant-based or regular Parmesan cheese, optional

Preheat the oven to 400°F (200°C). Dry the chickpeas with a clean tea towel, and then toss them in a bowl with the oil, dried wild garlic, and Himalayan salt, as needed. Spread the chickpeas out on a baking sheet lined with parchment paper and bake them in the oven for about 40 minutes. Turn them once or twice along the way.

While the chickpeas are baking, start the herb gravy. Boil the 2 cups (5 deciliters) of water in a saucepan, then add the bouillon, onion, herbs, and pepper. Let the gravy cook for 4 to 5 minutes, until the flavor develops. Season with more bouillon or herbs, if needed. Add cornstarch to the saucepan. Stir in a little at a time until the right consistency is reached. Stir constantly.

Heat up a large pan. Cut the pointed cabbage into quarters. When the pan is piping hot, lower the heat a little again and add the butter to the pan. Let it bubble up, then place the quartered pieces of cabbage in with the cut side down. Season with freshly ground Himalayan salt and pepper. Fry them about 5 to 7 minutes on each side until the cabbage has taken on a good color and is golden and tender.

Serve the cabbage on plates, drizzle with freshly squeezed lemon, grate parmesan cheese over the cabbage, if desired, or sprinkle with yeast flakes. Drizzle a bit of the herb gravy over the cabbage and top with a generous amount of crispy chickpeas.

REFRESHING SUMMER GAZPACHO

The taste of summer in a bowl. This simple, chilled vegetable soup filled with sun-ripened tomatoes, juicy cucumbers, and aromatic herbs and spices is perfect for warm days, when the long, soft rays of sun creep around us.

GAZPACHO
4 large sun-ripened tomatoes
1 peach
½ cucumber
¾ red onion
30 basil leaves
1½ teaspoons freshly ground
   Himalayan salt
1 tablespoon apple cider vinegar
½ teaspoon freshly ground
   pepper
1 tablespoon olive oil
1 teaspoon fresh chili, finely
   chopped

TOPPING
½ cucumber, diced
1 large tomato, diced
¼ red onion, diced
burrata, in coarse pieces
olive oil
½ avocado, sliced, optional

ADDITIONS
bread or baguette

Preheat the oven to 355°F (180°C). Blend all of the ingredients for the soup to the desired consistency. Season with the Himalayan salt, pepper, and herbs along the way. Warm the bread, and in the meantime, prepare the cucumber, tomato, red onion, and any avocado for topping. Arrange the gazpacho in deep plates, top with the vegetables, herbs, burrata, and freshly ground pepper. Drizzle with a good olive oil and eat with warm bread.

RAINBOW TART

At the end of the rainbow awaits this brightly colored and tempting tart filled with soft
herb mascarpone and luscious vegetables. A meal that will nourish your insides and
send your mood barometer sky high.

FOR 2–4 PEOPLE

TART CRUST
1½ cups (125 grams) gluten-
   free rolled oats
¾ cup (125 grams) whole grain
   rice flour
½ cup (1 deciliter) sesame
   seeds
2 eggs
1 teaspoon freshly ground
   Himalayan salt
¼ cup (½ deciliter) olive oil
¼–½ cup (½–1 deciliter) water

VEGETABLE FILLING
1 zucchini, in wide strips
1 sweet potato, in wide strips

**1 EGGPLANT, IN WIDE
STRIPS**
MASCARPONE CREAM
1⅛ cups (250 grams) plant-
   based or regular mascarpone
   cheese
1 portion gremolata-inspired
   herbal oil (see recipe on
   page 195)

OTHER
plant-based or churned butter

Blend the rolled oats into fine flour in a food processor. Then add the remaining ingredients for the tart crust, except the water, and blend to a crumbly dough. Add water, little by little, until the dough becomes soft and pliable. Roll out the dough evenly. Carefully place the tart dough in a greased tart pan and poke holes in it with a fork. Prebake the crust for about 10 minutes at 400°F (200°C).

Cut the vegetables into about ⅜-inch- (½-centimeter-) thick strips and place them on a baking sheet with parchment paper. Bake them together with the tart crust until almost tender but still with a slight bite. Meanwhile, blend the ingredients for the gremolata-inspired oil, and season to taste. Fold the herbal oil into the mascarpone and stir well.

When the tart crust is prebaked, spread the mascarpone cream on the crust in an even layer. Then decorate with the vegetable strips and make a rose or rainbow. Bake off the tart for about 20 to 30 minutes, or until the vegetables are cooked through.

RED WINE–BAKED MELTING CABBAGE

with marinated vegetable sausages

This melt-on-the-tongue cabbage is perfect for a Sunday evening, where time stands still, relaxation is total, and everyday trivial tasks are put on pause. Enjoy it with an extra good glass of red wine.

RED WINE–BAKED CABBAGE

1 large purple pointed cabbage, in wedges

2 onions, divided into wedges

8 cloves garlic, coarsely chopped

1 cup (2½ deciliters) vegetable stock

1 cup (2½ deciliters) red wine

3–4 dried bay leaves

1 large handful of fresh thyme, coarsely chopped

1 tablespoon chili flakes

white wine vinegar

coconut oil, for roasting

freshly ground Himalayan salt and pepper

SAUSAGES

8 vegetable sausages, divided into coarse pieces

VINAIGRETTE

1 tablespoon yellow mustard seeds

3 tablespoons apple cider vinegar

1 tablespoon olive oil

1 tablespoon honey

¼ teaspoon freshly ground Himalayan salt

¼ teaspoon freshly ground pepper

¼ cup (½ deciliter) fresh chives, finely chopped

Preheat the oven to 350°F (175°C). Cut the purple pointed cabbage into eight equal-sized wedges, and remove the center vein, if desired. Heat a little coconut oil in a heavy-bottomed pot so the entire bottom is covered. Sprinkle well with the Himalayan salt, pepper, and ½ tablespoon chili flakes over the oil and mix well. Fry the cabbage wedges on each cut surface until each side turns golden, transfer them to a large ovenproof dish, and drizzle a little white wine vinegar over them.

Cut the onions into wedges and coarsely chop the garlic. Reuse the pot from before and sauté the onion and garlic in coconut oil until they turn slightly golden. Add the vegetable stock, red wine, ¼ teaspoon Himalayan salt, bay leaves, and fresh thyme. Bring the pot to a gentle boil and turn off the burner.

Transfer the contents of the pot to the ovenproof dish and bake the cabbage for about 1 hour and 15 minutes.

Meanwhile, make the vinaigrette and set it aside.

When the cabbage is almost done, fry the sausages in a pan until they become slightly crisp. Serve the cabbage and sausages on dishes and pour the vinaigrette over the sausages just before serving.

HEARTWARMING EGGPLANT LASAGNA

There are countless selections of the Italian specialty, lasagna. Those with meat, and those with vegetables. Those with béchamel sauce, and those with mozzarella cheese. Those with salmon and Mornay sauce, and the ones I don't even know about or have tried, yet. Everyone has their very own favorite, or several, and here, I share one of mine that I think deserves a place in this book.

BAKED EGGPLANT

3 large eggplants, cut into
   ½-inch (1½-centimeter) slices
2 tablespoons olive oil
freshly ground Himalayan salt

SPINACH FILLING

2 onions, finely chopped
2 cloves garlic, finely chopped
5 cups (150 grams) baby spinach
1 tablespoon coconut oil
freshly ground Himalayan salt
   and pepper

RICOTTA FILLING

1 cup (250 grams) plant-based
   or regular ricotta cheese
1 egg
½ cup (1 deciliter) tightly packed
   basil leaves, chopped
1 teaspoon freshly ground
   Himalayan salt
1 teaspoon nutmeg, grated
½ teaspoon freshly ground
   pepper

Preheat the oven to 400° (200°C). Meanwhile, cut the eggplants into slices and distribute them over two baking sheets with parchment paper. Sprinkle the slices with Himalayan salt, turn them over, and salt the other side, as well. Let them stand for 15 to 20 minutes on the table until they start to "sweat" and release the bitter flavor. Pat them dry with a clean tea towel and brush them with olive oil. Turn them over and do the same on the opposite side. Bake them in the middle of the oven for 30–40 minutes until they're golden and tender.

While the eggplant is baking, make the spinach filling. Sauté the onion and garlic in coconut oil in a pan over medium heat until translucent, golden, and tender. Add the fresh spinach leaves and gently fold the mixture. Season with Himalayan salt and pepper. Turn off the heat and set the filling aside.

Add all the ingredients for the ricotta filling to a bowl and whisk with a fork. Set the mixture aside.

Also, make a portion of the marinara sauce so it's ready for assembling the lasagna.

LAYERS, FILLING, AND TOPPING

1 portion marinara sauce (see recipe on page 155)

1 portion arugula-almond pesto (see recipe on page 208)

8–10 pieces gluten-free lasagna sheets

1½ cups (200 grams) plant-based or regular mozzarella, grated

½–1 cup (50–100 grams) plant-based or regular Parmesan cheese or ½ cup (1 deciliter) yeast flakes

chili flakes

SERVING

with a good salad, optional

Spray or brush an ovenproof dish about 9 × 13 inches (23 × 33 centimeters) with olive or coconut oil. Spread ¾ to 1¼ cups (2 to 3 deciliters) of marinara sauce over the bottom so it's covered. Place a layer of lasagna sheets. Spread another portion of marinara sauce over the lasagna sheets so they're just lightly covered. The next layer consists of half the eggplant slices. They may overlap each other a bit if they're hard to fit in there. Spread half of the ricotta mixture over the eggplant slices and spread the spinach mixture evenly over that. Top with ¾ cup (2 deciliters) grated plant-based or regular mozzarella and a handful of grated Parmesan cheese. Place yet another layer of lasagna sheets and cover lightly with a portion of marinara sauce. There should be enough left for a final top layer on the lasagna. Distribute the last of the eggplant slices over the dish and cover them with the last portion of marinara sauce. Spread the remaining ricotta mixture out into soft pillows over the top, sprinkle with the remaining plant-based or regular mozzarella and a handful of grated Parmesan cheese or yeast flakes.

Bake the lasagna for about 50 minutes at 375°F (190°C). Depending on the oven, the lasagna may be baked covered with foil for the first half hour to prevent the cheese from becoming too runny.

While the lasagna is baking, make the arugula-almond pesto. The lasagna is ready when it's golden, bubbly, and slightly raised in the middle. Let it rest for 5 minutes before serving, and top with the arugula-almond-pesto. Serve with a good salad, if desired.

QUICK AND EASY MARINARA SAUCE

Quick and easy tomato sauce that can be created without a lot of arm movement. There is something so satisfying about making your own tomato sauce. Although it's one of the simplest things you can cook in the kitchen, there is a big difference between fresh tomatoes as the base or a can from the supermarket. This sauce is full of flavor, but I'd also invite you to explore the spice cabinet or kitchen garden to see if there's any extra magic the sauce needs to be supplemented with. Because we need to taste food so it suits us.

INGREDIENTS
2 pounds (1 kilogram) fresh tomatoes, halved or quartered
1 onion, finely chopped
4–6 cloves garlic, finely chopped
¼ teaspoon chili flakes
¼ cup (½ deciliter) fresh oregano, pinched
½ cup (1 deciliter) tomato puree
½ cup (1 deciliter) fresh basil leaves, chopped
3 tablespoons honey
coconut oil, for sautéing
balsamic vinegar
freshly ground Himalayan salt and pepper

Blend the fresh tomatoes in a blender. Sauté the onion and garlic in a saucepan with coconut oil over medium heat until they're soft and translucent. Add the chili flakes and oregano and stir. Pour in the blended tomatoes, add the tomato puree, and season with Himalayan salt and pepper. Let the sauce simmer for about 10 minutes, stirring regularly, until the sauce starts to thicken. Add the chopped basil leaves and season with the honey, balsamic vinegar, Himalayan salt, and pepper.

If the sauce becomes too thin, it needs to cook a little longer. If, on the other hand, it's too thick, it can be diluted with a little water.

Serve it with pasta, as pizza sauce, or with the eggplant lasagna that you'll also find here in the book.

The sauce can easily be frozen and reheated on busy weekdays.

THAI-INSPIRED COCONUT CAULIFLOWER SOUP

Take a trip to Thailand with this aromatic simmered dish. The fusion of greens, hot spices, and the rich base of coconut milk always gives me small flashbacks to my unforgettable travels around Asia, where I constantly encountered a playful collaboration of sweet, sharp, mild, and hot flavors.

SOUP

1 large onion, finely chopped

3 cloves garlic, finely chopped

2 celery sticks, sliced

1¼ cups (100 grams) shiitake mushrooms, sliced

½ head cauliflower, in small florets

1½ red peppers, in thin, bite-sized slices

1 red chili, seeded and finely chopped

1 tablespoon fresh ginger, finely grated

1 stalk fresh lemongrass

2 cans full fat coconut milk

1–2 teaspoons red curry paste

2 tablespoons coconut aminos

2 tablespoons sesame oil

fresh lime juice

¾ cup (200 milliliters) water + 1 tablespoon bouillon

coconut oil, for sautéing

freshly ground Himalayan salt and pepper

TOPPINGS AND ADDITIONS

fresh cilantro

fresh lime juice

freshly ground pepper

noodles and fresh lime slices, optional

Heat the coconut oil in a large pot. Sauté the onion and garlic until golden and translucent in color, then mix in the chopped chili. Add the celery, cauliflower, mushrooms, and red pepper, and sauté until slightly tender but not too brown.

Remove the tough outer layer from the lemongrass stalk and mash the stalk with a knife or rolling pin to release the aroma and flavors. Then cut it into thin slices.

Add the bouillon water, coconut milk, coconut aminos, ginger, lemongrass, and red curry paste to the soup. Bring to a boil and simmer over low heat for 15 to 20 minutes, or until the vegetables are slightly tender but still have bite.

Season with the sesame oil, lime juice, freshly ground salt, and pepper. If you have fresh cilantro left over, you can coarsely chop a handful and add it to the soup.

If you want, you can serve the soup with noodles, but it also tastes good as it is. Top with the fresh cilantro, freshly squeezed lime juice, freshly ground pepper, and the optional noodles and fresh lime slices.

CREAMY CASHEW BUTTERNUT SQUASH PASTA

with fried sage leaves

A simple pasta nestled under a deep orange, creamy blanket of umami, accompanied by a crispy crunch on top. A dish that invites you to an evening with bare toes in the grass, chilled white wine in a glass, and a sunset on the horizon.

CASHEW-BUTTERNUT SQUASH SAUCE

½ butternut squash
3 cloves garlic
1 onion, in wedges
½ cup (1 deciliter) cashews, soaked
1¼ cups (3 deciliters) water
1–2 teaspoons bouillon
a little grated nutmeg
1 tablespoon yeast flakes
1 teaspoon white wine vinegar
chili flakes
olive oil
freshly ground Himalayan salt and pepper

Turn on the oven to 400°F (200°C). Peel the butternut squash, cut it into bite-sized pieces, and toss the pieces in a little olive oil. Season with Himalayan salt. Then prepare the other ingredients. Place the butternut squash, onion, and garlic on a baking sheet lined with parchment paper and bake in the oven for about 40 minutes.

Add the pasta to some water and cook it al dente. While the pasta is cooking, heat a pan well and flash toast the walnuts until they're golden. Coarsely chop them and set them aside. Keep the pan on the heat, add a little olive oil, and fry the sage leaves for about 30 to 60 seconds until crisp, just until the point where they still retain the green color. Place them on a paper towel to absorb the fat from the leaves. Season with Himalayan salt.

ADDITIONS

1–1¼ cups (200–250 grams) pasta

10–15 sage leaves

½ cup (1 deciliter) walnuts, coarsely chopped

½ lemon, juice

chili flakes

plant-based or regular Parmesan cheese or yeast flakes, to taste

When the vegetables are finished baking and have a slightly caramelized surface, they're ready to be blended. Boil the 1⅔ cups (3 deciliters) of water and mix in the bouillon. Add the roasted vegetables, cashews, yeast flakes, white wine vinegar, and bouillon to the blender and blend until the sauce is creamy. Add more water along the way, if needed. Season with the grated nutmeg, Himalayan salt, and pepper. If a more intense flavor is desired, a few sage leaves can also be added to the sauce.

Drain the pasta. When the sauce has been seasoned, fold it into the pot with the pasta. Serve with chili flakes, toasted walnuts, a little freshly squeezed lemon juice, fried sage leaves, and the optional grated Parmesan cheese or yeast flakes.

SUMMER SALAD

with honey-roasted walnuts and herbal vinegar dressing

Sun, summer, and lots of salad. Embrace summer's beautiful raw materials with a wonderful and flavorful salad for warm barbecue evenings on the terrace in good company, or as a simple and light lunch on lazy weekdays.

HOMEMADE PICKLED BEETS

4 medium-sized beets, baked but still with bite, peeled, and diced or sliced
1 cup (2½ deciliters) vinegar
1 cup (2½ deciliters) water
¼–½ cup (½–1 deciliter) honey
1 teaspoon freshly ground Himalayan salt
¼ teaspoon mustard powder
1 teaspoon whole peppercorns

SALAD

¾ cup (100 grams) fresh strawberries, sliced
1⅓ cups (100 grams) fresh spinach leaves
5 cups (100 grams) fresh arugula
1⅛ cups (120 grams) goat feta or regular feta, crumbled over the salad

1 large handful mint leaves, chopped
1¼ cups (3 deciliters) homemade pickled beets, diced or sliced

HONEY ROASTED WALNUTS

1 cup (100 grams) walnuts, coarsely chopped
2 tablespoons honey
1 tablespoon churned or plant-based butter

HERBAL VINEGAR DRESSING

See recipe on page 210

Start by making the homemade pickled beets, if you don't already have a jar in the fridge. Heat a pot and boil the vinegar, water, honey, Himalayan salt, and mustard powder. Stir until the sugar is dissolved. Let it simmer for a bit, then take the pot off the heat so the mixture can cool down. Fill a 34-ounce (1-liter) sterile jar with a tight-fitting lid with the beets and peppercorns. Pour the vinegar mixture over the beets to cover them. Let them stand and infuse for half a day—and preferably up to 24 hours—after which the jar is stored in the fridge.

Mix all of the ingredients for the salad in a bowl. Heat a pan, then add the butter. Toast the walnuts in the butter until they take on a little color. Then pour the honey over and fold the walnuts until the butter and honey are mixed well. Remove the pan from the burner and let the walnuts cool on a plate before topping the salad with them along with the herbal vinegar dressing.

Sweet and savory treats

We all deserve a little pampering while we take time for ourselves to reminisce, gather, or discover new things about each other. Regardless of whether the desire is for the soft, the crunchy, the snackable, the fresh, the warm, or the chilled, there are plenty of options to choose from.

LUXURY TRUFFLES

Rum balls, crumb balls, bliss balls, date balls, or truffles. A beloved child has many names. These small balls of chocolate delight melt on the tongue, grease the fingers, and take your smile to new heights.

TRUFFLES

⅔ cup (150 grams) sugar-free marzipan

¾ cup (2 deciliters) hazelnuts

5 Medjool dates, pitted

1 tablespoon raw cacao powder

1 teaspoon reishi powder

¼ teaspoon ground cardamom

1½ teaspoons ground Ceylon cinnamon

1 teaspoon vanilla extract

¼ teaspoon freshly ground Himalayan salt

½ teaspoon ground cloves

½ teaspoon ground ginger

¼ teaspoon ground allspice

¼ cup + 1 tablespoon (40 grams) dark
chocolate

2 tablespoons orange juice, freshly
squeezed

pinch ground chili

TOPPING

raw cacao powder

freeze-dried fruit

Blend all of the ingredients into a
smooth mass in a food processor. Roll
into balls and roll them in raw cacao
powder and freeze-dried fruit. Can be
stored in the fridge and in the freezer if
they don't manage to be eaten before.

MATCHA RAW-CAKE BITES

Green is the new black, and it's hard to get over the fact that even though the pretty neon green color enchants the eye, matcha's distinct flavor can take some getting used to for some. Here, the magical green tea unfolds in a different flavor combination than the classic, well-known latte.

ABOUT 6–8 PIECES

CRUST

1 cup (150 grams) Medjool dates, pitted
¾ cup (2 deciliters) gluten-free rolled oats
½ cup (1 deciliter) almonds, toasted
2 tablespoons hemp seeds
½ teaspoon freshly ground Himalayan salt
1 teaspoon lucuma powder
1 tablespoon tahini
1 tablespoon coconut oil
½ cup (1 deciliter) coconut, grated
2 tablespoons raw cacao powder

MATCHA CREAM

1¼ cups (3 deciliters) cashew nuts, soaked
2 teaspoons high-quality matcha powder
¼–½ cup (½–1 deciliter) lemon juice, depending on how acidic the bites should be
3 tablespoons coconut oil
⅔ cup (1½ deciliters) coconut cream, the fat portion
2 tablespoons agave syrup
1 teaspoon vanilla extract
2 teaspoons lime zest, grated
1 tablespoon lime juice, freshly squeezed

TOPPING

pistachios, coarsely chopped

Heat up a pan and toast the almonds until golden. Blend all of the ingredients for the crust in a food processor. Line a square baking dish with parchment paper or spray the bottom and edges with coconut oil. Distribute the mixture in the baking dish and press it flat and even. Clean the bowl of the food processor and prepare the ingredients for the matcha cream. Blend all of the ingredients and flavor with the lemon juice, lime zest, vanilla extract, and maple syrup, depending on how sweet or acidic you want the cream to be. When it is absolutely perfect, spread the cream over the date crust in an even layer. Place the cake in the freezer for 4 to 6 hours.

Take the cake out and let it stand for 15 to 30 minutes before cutting it into bite-sized pieces or larger chunks. Freeze them again, and then there's always a little something to grab, should the sweet tooth show up.

SEASONED POPCORN IN 3 VERSIONS

Crispy, crunchy popcorn has to be, undoubtedly, the snack of a lifetime. In recent years, the popped corn kernels have had a bit of a renaissance and something of an upgrade compared to the ones you know from the dark movie theater and the microwave. Now, they're available in new, exciting flavors, and you can easily imitate art at home.

Homemade popcorn made in a pot on the stove is just healthier than the ones that are popped in a bag in the microwave. The ingredients are simple and you avoid artificial flavors and preservatives. You can season them however you like and pop them in your favorite oil. Below, you will find my basic recipe, including three seasoning mixes you can top it with. It yields 1 to 2 servings of each mix, but you can always double or triple the mixes so you have them longer. Just remember to store the seasoning mixes in an airtight container in a dark place.

MAIN INGREDIENTS
⅔ cup (1½ deciliters) popcorn
   kernels
2 tablespoons coconut oil

THE UMAMI MIX
1 tablespoon dried dill
1 teaspoon dried thyme
1 teaspoon onion powder
⅛–¼ teaspoon freshly ground
   Himalayan salt
2 tablespoons yeast flakes, to
   top

THE TANGY MIX
½ teaspoon onion powder
½ teaspoon garlic powder
2 teaspoons ground cilantro
2 teaspoons dried dill
⅛–¼ teaspoon freshly ground
   Himalayan salt
½ teaspoon ground mustard
   powder
¼ teaspoon citric acid

THE RANCH MIX
½ teaspoon garlic powder
½ teaspoon onion powder
2 teaspoons dried parsley
2 teaspoons dried dill
⅛–¼ teaspoon freshly ground
   Himalayan salt
½ teaspoon freshly ground
   pepper

Melt one heaping tablespoon of coconut oil over medium heat in a heavy-bottomed pot. Pour the popcorn kernels into the pot so they cover the bottom and put the lid on. The kernels should only be in one layer and not cover each other. When the kernels start to pop, open the lid slightly so that the steam can seep out. This prevents the popcorn from becoming soft and chewy. Shake the pot at regular intervals (about every 10 seconds) until the popping subsides again.

Take the lid off the pot, coat the popcorn with a little oil (possibly using spray), and season with one of the three seasoning mixes.

CHOCOLATE GANACHE

with rose petals and reishi

*A sinful, rich, and seductive little thing that literally melts on the tongue and that I almost
dare to swear can excite the palate of even the most critical chocolate connoisseur. Let this
dark dream complete a magical dinner party with those you care about.*

ABOUT 10–12 PEOPLE

CRUST
½ cup (1 deciliter) coconut oil, melted
2 cups (5 deciliters) hazelnuts
⅔ cup (1½ deciliters) almonds
6 tablespoons coconut sugar
1 teaspoon freshly ground Himalayan salt
10 Medjool dates, pitted

CHOCOLATE GANACHE
1⅓ cups (200 grams) sugar-free dark chocolate, chopped
1 can fat coconut cream
¼ cup (½ deciliter) coconut oil, melted
1 teaspoon vanilla powder
1 teaspoon ground cardamom
1 teaspoon ground Ceylon cinnamon
2 tablespoons powdered reishi
coconut sugar to sweeten

TOPPING
rose petals and buds
cocoa nibs
salt flakes

Preheat the oven to 350°F (175°C). Grease or spray a springform pan about 9½ inches (24 centimeters) in diameter with coconut oil. Blend all of the ingredients for the crust in a food processor until the nuts are chopped well. Transfer the nut mixture to the springform pan and spread the mixture evenly on the bottom. Press down so the mixture becomes firm. Bake the crust in the oven for about 30 to 40 minutes, until golden brown. Depending on how thick the crust is, it may need to come out of the oven earlier so it doesn't burn. Then set the crust aside to cool.

While the crust is baking, prepare the chocolate ganache. Place the chopped chocolate in a bowl along with the melted coconut oil. Heat the coconut cream in a small saucepan over medium heat until it begins to simmer, then pour it over the chocolate. Stir until the chocolate melts into the coconut cream and the mixture becomes nice and creamy. Add the vanilla powder, cardamom, reishi, and cinnamon, and flavor it with coconut sugar. Pour the chocolate-coconut cream over the nut crust in the spring form pan and refrigerate for at least 1 hour.

When the cake has set, loosen it from the sides of the pan with a wet, sharp knife. Garnish with rose petals and buds, cocoa nibs, and salt flakes before serving.

CRISPY VEGETABLE SNACKS

Crispy little snacks that crunch between the teeth and have great flavor. Beautiful as a topping for salads and soup, or in a little handful when the afternoon crisis hits the small tummies. Before you know it, this batch may already be gone, so be sure to have a little extra in stock so you can quickly whip up a new round.

ABOUT 1 BAKING SHEET

INGREDIENTS
10–12 radishes, thinly sliced

1 can chickpeas, drained and rinsed

1½ cups (150 grams) fresh baby sprouts, rinsed

2 teaspoons dried thyme

2 teaspoons dried rosemary

1 teaspoon fennel seeds

1 teaspoon dried parsley

1 teaspoon chili flakes

1 teaspoon freshly ground Himalayan salt

2 tablespoons olive oil

Preheat the oven to 355°F (180°C). Mix all of the ingredients in a bowl and turn well with your hands so the oil and spices are distributed evenly. Spread a piece of parchment paper on a baking sheet and spread the mixture out. Leave some elbow room for the vegetables so the baking sheet isn't overcrowded. Bake for 30 to 40 minutes, or until the vegetables are crisp and golden. Keep an eye on them along the way and turn them over with a spatula.

Serve them right away and store the rest in an airtight container.

ALMOND COOKIES
with cashew-rose cream

Some days can be gray, boring, and long. But you can decide for yourself whether you want to turn the day around and make it full of pampering and home baking!

COOKIES
2 cups (5 deciliters) almond flour
2 cups (5 deciliters) gluten-free
   oat flour
½ cup (1 deciliter) coconut sugar
⅔ cup (1½ deciliter) coconut oil,
   melted
2 teaspoons vanilla powder or
   6 teaspoons vanilla extract
2 teaspoons baking powder
2 teaspoons freshly ground
   Himalayan salt
2 eggs
¾ cup (2 deciliters) pistachios,
   finely chopped

CASHEW-ROSE CREAM
1¼ cups (3 deciliters) cashews,
   soaked
¼ cup (½ deciliter) almond or
   cashew milk
¼ cup (½ deciliter) coconut oil,
   melted
2 tablespoons date syrup or agave
   syrup
3 teaspoons vanilla extract
¼–½ tablespoon rose water
1–2 teaspoons pink pitaya powder

TOPPING
rose petals

Preheat the oven to 350°F (175°C). Blend all of the ingredients for the cookies in a food processor. The dough should be moist and sticky. Divide the dough into 18 to 20 balls that are 1½ to 2 inches (4–5 centimeters) in diameter. Roll the chopped pistachios into the dough. Then shape the balls into cookies and place them on a baking sheet lined with parchment paper. Make a small indentation in the center of each cookie for the cashew-rose cream and pinch together any cracks in the edge of the cookie if they occur. Bake the cookies for about 20 minutes and keep an eye on them along the way so they don't overbake.

While the cookies are in the oven, make the cashew-rose cream. Blend all of the ingredients for the cream in a blender or food processor until the mixture is nice and smooth. If necessary, adjust the flavor along the way if you want the cream to taste more like rose water or be sweeter.

When the cookies are done baking, transfer them to a wire rack to cool. Then top each cookie with a scoop of cashew-rose cream and decorate with dried rose petals.

Refrigerate them in an airtight container for up to a week.

RAW COCONUT MACAROONS IN 3 VERSIONS

Let the sweet flavor of coconut ignite the feeling of happiness, while the small elements of surprise awaken your senses. Small, round treats you can enjoy when you need something sweet-but-not-too-sweet.

BASIC

3¼ cups (8 deciliters) coconut, grated
⅔ cup (1½ deciliters) coconut oil, melted
½ cup (1 deciliter) almond flour
2 tablespoons honey
4 scoops collagen powder
1 tablespoon vanilla extract
2 teaspoons reishi powder
½ teaspoon freshly ground Himalayan salt
¼ cup (½ deciliter) almond or soy cream

MATCHA-LIME

1 teaspoon high-quality matcha powder
2 teaspoons lime zest, finely grated
1 teaspoon lime juice, freshly squeezed

RASPBERRY-AÇAI

2 teaspoons açai powder
2 teaspoons pink pitaya powder
½ cup (70 grams) fresh raspberries

GINGER-TURMERIC-LEMON

1 teaspoon ground or fresh turmeric
2 teaspoons fresh ginger, finely grated
3 teaspoons lemon juice, freshly squeezed

Blend the ingredients for the basic ones in a food processor until everything is mixed well. Divide the dough among three bowls and add the matcha, lime zest, and lime juice to one bowl; the açai powder, pitaya powder, and fresh raspberries to the second bowl; and the turmeric, ginger, and lemon juice to the third bowl. Mix well and form 6 to 8 balls of each mixture. If you want a crispier surface, you can bake them in the oven for 15 to 20 minutes at 350°F (175°C). Otherwise, just put the macaroons in the refrigerator for at least 1 hour, after which they're ready to serve. They can also be frozen easily and grabbed when snack cravings strike.

PASTA CHIPS

Do you have leftover pasta that you don't quite know what to do with? Turn it into a
fun, crunchy, and delicious snack that can excite young and old.

ABOUT 3–4 SERVINGS

INGREDIENTS
2 cups (200 grams) gluten-free
   bow, penne, or rotini pasta
3 tablespoons olive oil
½ cup (1 deciliter) yeast flakes,
   or plant-based or regular
   Parmesan cheese, finely
   grated
1 teaspoon garlic powder
1 teaspoon dried parsley
1 teaspoon dried rosemary
1 teaspoon dried oregano
1 teaspoon freshly ground
   Himalayan salt
freshly ground pepper

Preheat the oven to 400°F (200 °C). Cook the pasta according to the package directions until al dente. Drain, and shake any remaining water out of the individual pieces of pasta. Do not let them dry completely or they'll stick together. Transfer the pasta to a bowl and toss in oil so each piece of pasta is well coated. Sprinkle with yeast flakes or Parmesan cheese, and season well with the garlic powder, parsley, rosemary, oregano, Himalayan salt, and pepper. Mix it one last time. Place the pasta on a baking sheet lined with parchment paper in a single layer and bake in the oven for about 25 to 30 minutes. Keep an eye on the pasta pieces along the way, and if they need more or less time, just adjust the baking time accordingly, since ovens are different.

Serve with your favorite dip or maybe even a marinara sauce.

SWEET AND SALTY HERBED NUTS

Although this recipe is simple, it is too good not to share. For cozy dining, a drink on the terrace, or just to satisfy hunger. But be careful! These nuts can be highly addictive.

FOR 1 LARGE BOWL

INGREDIENTS

1¼ cups (3 deciliters) walnuts, unsalted

1¼ cups (3 deciliters) cashews, unsalted

1¼ cups (3 deciliters) pecans, unsalted

2–3 tablespoons fresh rosemary leaves, finely chopped

1 tablespoon coconut sugar

½–1 teaspoon ground cayenne pepper

1 tablespoon flake salt

1 teaspoon ground Ceylon cinnamon

2 tablespoons plant-based or churned butter, melted

1 tablespoon maple syrup

Preheat the oven to 350°F (175°C). Mix the rosemary, coconut sugar, cayenne pepper, flake salt, and cinnamon in a small, separate bowl. Heat the butter and maple syrup in a small saucepan but be careful not to let the syrup start to crystallize. Transfer the butter and syrup mixture along with the nuts into a large bowl and mix the spice and coconut sugar mixture into it. Mix well. Spread the spiced nuts on a baking sheet lined with parchment paper and roast for about fifteen minutes, or until the nuts are lightly toasted. Turn them along the way. Allow them to cool completely before eating—preferably 2 hours or longer, so the flavor intensifies—and store them in an airtight container.

CHOCOLATE RICE CAKES
with crunch

A sweet and crunchy afternoon boost when the energy is about to run out. Try the composition below, or let your creative whim take you on new flavor adventures. Limited only by imagination.

CHOCOLATE RICE CAKES

10 rice cakes, unsalted
1 cup (150 grams) sugar-free
 dark chocolate, melted
2 teaspoons astragalus powder
2 teaspoons chaga powder

CRUNCH
bee pollen
hemp seeds
coconut flour
goji berries or mulberries
almonds, chopped

Start by making room in the refrigerator for a plate or a large cutting board. Place a piece of parchment paper on your chosen surface where the rice cakes can sit. Fill a shallow bowl with the melted chocolate and stir in the astragalus and chaga. If necessary, keep it warm in a water bath. Pick out the different crunch ingredients so they're ready to be sprinkled on. One by one, dip the rice cakes in the melted chocolate. Use a brush or similar to distribute the chocolate in the nooks of the rice cakes. Sprinkle the crunch over the rice cakes in the proportion you want. Remember, the different toppings should touch the melted chocolate to stick. Repeat the process with the remaining rice cakes. Refrigerate to set. The rice cakes taste best slightly chilled, so store them in the refrigerator.

Dips, toppings, and crunches

A sprinkle of love on top or a smooth dip for your crackers. Sometimes, it's just that extra something we crave with a meal, whether simple and easy or large and sumptuous, it makes a difference and satisfies all the senses.

GREMOLATA-INSPIRED HERBAL OIL

It's hard not to let your thoughts wander south to the boot country and its charming history and flavorful cuisine with this coarse gremolata-inspired herb oil. The sweetness from the honey plays elegantly against the bitter parsley and robust garlic. A breath of fresh air that can enliven even the most boring creation.

FOR 1 LARGE SERVING

INGREDIENTS
¾ cup (2 deciliters) fresh
   parsley
1–2 cloves garlic
1 teaspoon lemon zest, grated
1 tablespoon lemon juice,
   freshly squeezed
1 teaspoon honey
¼ cup (½ deciliter) olive oil
freshly ground Himalayan salt
   and pepper

Coarsely chop all of the ingredients in a mini chopper, and season with the garlic, lemon, Himalayan salt, and pepper along the way. The gremolata should be slightly coarse and with a slight bite. Pour the coarse herbal oil into a sanitized airtight jar and keep in the fridge.

GREEN TAHINI SAUCE

Our lush and generous nature is one big pantry that offers a multitude of green and flavorful surprises all year round that particularly flirt with our senses. A selection of greens is used in this recipe, and I would almost say that it's the flavor and aroma of summer poured into a glass. What more could you wish for?

YIELDS 1 PORTION

INGREDIENTS

1 tablespoon lemon juice, freshly squeezed

½ cup (1 deciliter) fresh cilantro

¾ cup (2 deciliters) fresh parsley

1 clove garlic

10 fresh mint leaves

30 fresh basil leaves

1 teaspoon freshly ground Himalayan salt

½ cup (1 deciliter) tahini

½ teaspoon fresh chili, finely chopped

⅔ cup (1½ deciliters) water

1 teaspoon honey

½ teaspoon lemon zest, grated

1 tablespoon olive oil

Blend all of the ingredients in a blender on high speed. Flavor the sauce as you go if it's missing more sweetness, bitterness, or strength.

COCONUT BACON

Crispy, smoky, salty, and umami. Look forward to tasting "the spice of life" in a new, delicious, and lighter interpretation, made with full-fat coconut flakes, smoked paprika, and lots of love.

INGREDIENTS
2 cups (5 deciliters) coconut flakes

1 tablespoon walnut oil

2 tablespoons tamari

1½ teaspoons ground smoked paprika

1 tablespoon maple syrup

1 teaspoon liquid smoke

1 dash freshly ground Himalayan salt

½ teaspoon freshly ground black pepper

Preheat the oven to 320°F (160°C) and place a piece of parchment paper on a baking sheet. Mix all of the ingredients in a bowl and toss the coconut flakes well with the water and spices.

Spread the mixture on the baking sheet in an even layer and bake for about 5 to 7 minutes. Give the mixture a good stir, then bake for another 5 to 7 minutes, or until the coconut flakes are toasted brown. Keep a close eye on them in the second round of baking, since they can quickly turn black and scorch if they're given too much time.

Take out the baking sheet, let the coconut flakes cool off, and notice how they now get even crispier. Store them in an airtight jar for up to a month. Use them as a topping on salads, sandwiches, soups, or something else entirely.

PÂTÉ

Bid the pâté a warm welcome in a greener guise. It can be used as a dip, spread, and snacked on, just the way you want.

INGREDIENTS

2 red onions, chopped

½ pound (250 grams) mixed mushrooms, chopped

1 tablespoon dark balsamic vinegar

3–4 cloves garlic, chopped

1 tablespoon fresh rosemary, chopped

1 tablespoon fresh thyme, chopped

1 cup (2½ deciliters) walnuts, toasted

1 handful fresh parsley, chopped

2 tablespoons white miso

½ teaspoon freshly ground black pepper

freshly ground Himalayan salt

coconut oil, for sautéing

Heat up a pan, grease well with coconut oil, and sauté the red onion and mushrooms until tender and the onions start to caramelize.

Add the tablespoon of dark balsamic vinegar, garlic, rosemary, and thyme. Continue to sauté for 3 to 5 minutes. Take the pan off the burner and let the vegetables cool down a bit.

Blend all of the ingredients in a food processor until the mixture becomes smooth and spreadable. Season with Himalayan salt, miso, or more herbs.

Serve on bread, as a dip for crackers, or as a side dish for dinner. Store the pâté in a sanitized jar in the refrigerator. It tastes best when it's been out for just a while and isn't completely refrigerator cold.

DANDELION SYRUP
with lavender

Turn spring and summer's worst adversaries into liquid and sweet floral gold that can be used in both savory and sweet cuisine. The beautiful yellow flowers, that are otherwise hated by many gardeners because they're difficult to overcome, contain some interesting floral notes that do particularly well in the gastronomic universe.

INGREDIENTS
90 dandelion heads, rinsed and cleaned
2 cups (½ liter) water
juice from ½ lemon
2 tablespoons dried lavender (optional)
3¾ cups (750 grams) unrefined cane sugar

Pinch all of the green from the dandelion heads, making sure you only have the yellow petals left. The green part contains a number of bitter substances that can make the flavor bitter.

Pour all of the leaves into a thick-bottomed saucepan together with the water, dried lavender, and juice from half a lemon. Let it simmer for about 30 minutes. Meanwhile, put a small plate in the refrigerator, which will be used later to check the syrup's consistency.

Then strain the liquid into another saucepan and add the unrefined cane sugar. Flavor with more lemon juice, if desired. Let the syrup boil down to the desired consistency, which can take up to 1 to 2 hours. Check the consistency continuously by placing a few drops on a chilled, small plate. If it runs a lot, the mixture needs to boil more, and if it firms slightly, that's a sign of a good consistency.

If your syrup becomes too thick, you can dilute it with more water. If it's too thin, then boil it some more.

Put the syrup in a sanitized jar or bottle, and it can easily keep for six months to an entire year.

WHAT IS AN OXYMEL?

An oxymel is an herbal mixture with honey and vinegar as a base. It can be good for lubricating the throat, relieving coughs, and helping the immune system during colds and flu. When the honey-vinegar mixture is combined with herbs that have similar properties, oxymel becomes a flavorful supplement for reducing discomfort. There are many ways to make an oxymel. Here, I have made a 1:2 ratio between honey and apple cider vinegar. Play around with the proportions, depending on which herbs you want to try out, and how strong or mild in taste you want it.

HOW TO HARVEST ELDERFLOWERS

If you're lucky enough to have an elder tree in your garden or nearby, be sure to harvest properly so you don't over-pick or damage the tree's flowering. Pick a maximum of 5 to 10 percent of the flowers on each tree. The flowers turn into elderberries later in the season, and we want to leave enough flowers so that the berries can grow. If you don't have a tree nearby, make sure you're not harvesting in a contaminated area that could leave toxins in the flowers.

ELDERFLOWER OXYMEL

An oxy-what? A simple but potent and particularly useful sweet-and-sour herbal mixture that can be used in everything from salads to drinks. The base consists of ingredients you may already have at home. It doesn't have to be more difficult to make magic in the kitchen.

INGREDIENTS

3 cups (7½ deciliters) elderflowers, cleaned and rinsed

1 cup (2½ deciliters) honey

2 cups (5 deciliters) apple cider vinegar

It is super easy to make an oxymel. Cut the flowers off the stems and fill a sanitized jar with them. Be sure the jar has a glass or plastic lid, because the vinegar can cause a metal lid to corrode. Pour the honey over and top the rest of the jar up with the apple cider vinegar. The honey makes the oxymel sweet and delicious if it is to be used in a drink.

Let your elderflower oxymel sit in a dark place and infuse for 3 to 4 weeks. When it's ready, pour it through a sieve into a sanitized jar. Use it as a dressing for salads, as a base for a cocktail, or just take a spoonful of it as it is. There are almost no limits to what it can be used for.

RUSTIC ARUGULA-ALMOND PESTO

The taste of sun, summer, and Italy in a little jar. Give new life to a dry piece of bread, whip up a quick pasta pesto on busy weekdays, or give your favorite dishes an extra notch up on the indulgence scale with a dollop of homemade pesto on top.

INGREDIENTS

⅔ cup (1½ deciliters) almonds, roasted

1 cup (2½ deciliters) fresh arugula

1 handful fresh basil

1 clove garlic

1 teaspoon lemon juice, freshly squeezed

⅔ cup (1½ deciliters) olive oil

freshly ground Himalayan salt and pepper

Chop all of the ingredients in a food processor or powerful mini chopper until everything is well mixed and finely chopped. Add more oil to achieve a smoother pesto and some more almonds for a more rustic consistency. The pesto can be stored in the fridge for 4 to 5 days.

MINI GUIDE:
MIX YOUR OWN
HERBAL VINEGAR DRESSING

It's easy to make your own herbal vinegar dressing, and it can quickly become a dear friend to have sitting in the kitchen all year round, when there's just a dressing missing on the salad, a marinade for the vegetables, or extra flavor in the soup.

As I have mentioned many times before, nature's herbs are a gift to the kitchen, our well-being, and the culinary experience. One of the easiest ways to preserve the nutrition profile of the herbs is by making an herbal vinegar dressing.

Depending on the ratio between the amount of herbs and vinegar, as well as how long you choose to let the herbal vinegar infuse, you get a milder or stronger herbal vinegar dressing. If you choose 2 to 3 sprigs of the fresh herb and store them in vinegar in a jar, you get a subtle herb flavor. If you choose a larger portion of herbs in relation to the vinegar, it leaves a strong flavor of herbs, with the vinegar as the secondary flavor.

There are also two ways you can preserve herbs in vinegar.

THE SLOW METHOD

1. Lightly crush the herb's leaves and transfer them to a sanitized jar or bottle.
2. Add your vinegar of choice. Be sure the herbs are fully covered. Put the lid on. A plastic lid or glass lid is best, because metal lids can corrode.
3. Store the jar or bottle in a dark place for up to 6 to 8 weeks. You can then decant the vinegar or let the herbs remain in the vinegar.

THE FASTER METHOD

1. Heat the vinegar up in a saucepan to just below the boiling point. It must not boil, but should just heat up.
2. Put a suitable amount of herbs in a sanitized jar or bottle, and pour the hot vinegar over until the herbs are covered.
3. Put the lid on, and store in a dark place for 3 to 4 weeks. You can then decant the vinegar or let the herbs remain in the vinegar.

Use this mini guide to put together your own herbal vinegar dressing. Always remember to wash, clean, and dry the ingredients well so there are no brown spots and bad parts on your herbs, fruits, or vegetables.

Use 1 part fresh herbs, fruits, roots, bark, or a mix of these, to 2 parts vinegar. For 1 part of dried herbs, use 15 parts of vinegar. You can always play with the ratio between herbs, fruits, and vegetables, depending on how sweet or spicy you want your herbal vinegar dressing. Let the mixture infuse for 3 to 4 weeks and up to 6 to 8 weeks.

You may experience finding a film that forms at the top of your jar, either while the vinegar is steeping, or after it has been decanted. Although it is not dangerous, it indicates that the vinegar is entering the next fermentation stage, which can change the vinegar's flavor and texture. To take the best care of your herbal vinegar dressing, you can remove the film with wooden tongs or clean hands.

RAVISHING GARDEN HERBS

Oregano, thyme, basil, rosemary, wild garlic, dill, sage, bay leaves, mint, lemongrass, lemon balm, chives, lovage, and tarragon.

FRESH FRUIT

Raspberries, blueberries, blackberries, cranberries, strawberries, elderberries, peaches, nectarines, apricots, cherries, pineapples, rhubarb, and zest from citrus fruits.

GENEROUS VEGETABLES

Onion, green onion, dried red pepper, and hot pepper or chili.

ADVENTUROUS VINEGARS

There are a multitude of vinegars on the market. Go for one that is 5 percent acidity or more.

Red Wine Vinegar—Deep in flavor and goes well with strong herbs like rosemary, but unfortunately, this vinegar has a tendency to mask the flavor of more subtle herbs, like thyme.

White Wine Vinegar—Delicate in flavor and goes well with mild herbs and fruit, like peaches.

Apple Cider Vinegar—Full of flavor and works well with fruit and herbs, like rosemary.

Champagne Vinegar—Delicate in flavor and goes well with mild herbs and fruit, like peaches.

Balsamic Vinegar—Deep in flavor and is well-stimulated with strong herbs and spices, like rosemary, but this vinegar also has a tendency to mask the flavor of more subtle herbs.

SPICES WITH EDGE

You can easily make an herbal vinegar dressing without extra spices, but adding a spice or two can lift the mixture to a whole new level. Use the spices in their whole form (not ground), since it makes it easier to strain them out afterwards.

Black pepper, mustard seed, clove, cinnamon stick, star anise, fresh garlic clove, and fresh ginger root.

ESSENTIAL EQUIPMENT

Pot, funnel, glass jars with tight-fitting lid (not metal), mixing glass, sieve or nut milk bag, and possibly rubber bands and manila tags to note what's in your herbal vinegar dressing and when it was made.

SPICY HERBAL VINEGAR DRESSING

apple cider vinegar
tarragon, chive, or lemon balm
hot pepper, garlic, and/or chili
clove and peppercorn

FRESH HERBAL VINEGAR DRESSING

red wine vinegar
lemon thyme and mint leaves
garlic, ginger root, and lemongrass

FRUITY HERBAL VINEGAR DRESSING

champagne vinegar
rose petals, lemon thyme, and lemon
  balm
peaches and zest from one lemon

THE ROBUST HERBAL VINEGAR DRESSING

red wine vinegar
rosemary, oregano, thyme, and garlic
raspberry
a small mixture of clove, allspice, black
  peppercorn, cardamom seeds, nutmeg,
  and cinnamon stick

THE LIGHT HERBAL VINEGAR DRESSING

white wine vinegar
dill, garlic, and mint
blueberries and zest from one lemon
clove and black peppercorn

VERSATILE HERBAL SALT

with rosemary, thyme, and citrus

*Here is the recipe for a little spiced wonder for the kitchen. It can perk up any everyday
dish, and also makes an excellent hostess gift for the food enthusiasts in your life.*

INGREDIENTS

2 cups (5 deciliters) Himalayan
    salt, sea salt, or salt flakes,
    not-too-coarse pieces

4 tablespoons fresh rosemary
    leaves, finely chopped

1 tablespoon fresh thyme
    leaves, finely chopped

6 oranges, blood oranges, or
    lemons, juice from 2 and zest
    from 6

Preheat the oven to 210°F (100°C). Mix the salt,
rosemary, and thyme in a bowl. Remove the zest from
the citrus fruit and cut it into small strips. Avoid getting
the white pith under the zest with it. Squeeze the juice
out of 2 of the citrus fruits and turn it with the citrus zest
in the bowl with the salt. Distribute the mixture on a
baking sheet with parchment paper, and bake for about
45 to 60 minutes, or until the salt is no longer moist.
Turn the mixture continuously. The salt mixture must not
turn dark or sweat. Crumble any clumps loose with a
wooden spoon and store the salt in an airtight container
for up to 3 months.

Sprinkle it on seafood, vegetables, or even over the
Friday popcorn.

Cool and warm temptations

Do you remember to celebrate yourself and those you care about in everyday life? Not just the big events that are worth celebrating with flags and that bring tears of joy to the corner of the eye, but also the small moments of happiness in everyday life: A warm June evening on the terrace after a brisk summer shower, when your favorite song is playing on the radio for the last hour of the work day, or when you have a row of green lights and can cycle in third gear all the way home. Life's small moments are what happen when we are present in the now. Celebrate big, small, and just because with a warm cup of your favorite latte or with clinking glasses filled with mouthwatering, cool refreshments.

FIRE CIDER TONIC

This immune-boosting drink becomes a dear friend in times of need, especially in the cold winter months, when many of us are ailing a little extra. It's based on apple cider vinegar, which gives a loving nudge to slow digestion, and the remaining ingredients make the flavor strong, sour, slightly earthy, and with a little hint of sweetness. Individually and together, the ingredients give the drink a number of good properties, including being anti-inflammatory, antibacterial, detoxifying, and digestion-stimulating.

Take 1 to 2 tablespoons daily and increase the intake if you feel a cold coming on. If you find it difficult to drink it straight, you can mix a few spoonsful in a warm ginger tea, pour it over salads as a vinaigrette, or mix it into soups and stews.

INGREDIENTS

2 small onions, chopped

1 head garlic, peeled and lightly mashed

2 jalapeños, tops cut off and chopped

⅔ cup (1½ deciliters) fresh horseradish, grated

⅔ cup (1½ deciliters) fresh ginger, grated

⅔ cup (1½ deciliters) fresh turmeric, grated

2 oranges, juice and grated zest

1 lemon, juice and grated zest

1 cinnamon stick

1 handful black peppercorns

1 small teaspoon ground cayenne pepper

¼ cup (½ deciliter) raw honey

apple cider vinegar

Grate the turmeric, ginger, the zest of the citrus fruit, and horseradish. Coarsely chop the onion and garlic. Squeeze the juice out of the citrus fruit, then mix all of the ingredients in a large airtight and sanitized jar, about 34 ounces (1 liter), in the following order: onion and garlic, grated ginger, grated horseradish, grated turmeric, lemon zest and orange zest, juice from the citrus fruits, jalapeños, peppercorns, cinnamon stick, and cayenne pepper. Top the ingredients with apple cider vinegar and close the jar with a lid. Store the jar in a cool, dark place for about 1 month. Shake the jar daily to make sure the ingredients are mixed well. Then sieve the mixture and mix in honey to taste. Store the tonic in the fridge.

MOUTHWATERING MOCKTAILS

Bare shoulders peeking out. The smell of grilled vegetables wafts into the air. The ice cubes clink in the glass, and the mood barometer climbs a few degrees. We all know those summer evenings when we get together with good friends over a drink and forget everything around us for awhile. Here are three good selections for alcohol-free cocktails full of juice and energy.

GRAPEFRUIT, CLEMENTINE, AND ROSEMARY

ABOUT 2 GLASSES

1 grapefruit, peeled, and the membrane peeled off around the individual segments

2 clementines, peeled, and the membrane peeled off around the individual segments

1 teaspoon fresh rosemary, finely chopped

2 teaspoons honey

1 tablespoon apple cider vinegar

1 teaspoon fresh ginger, grated

sparkling water (with or without citrus)

ice cubes

Blend all of the ingredients into a creamy juice without clumps. Divide the juice into two glasses with ice cubes, and top with sparkling water.

HIBISCUS-CILANTRO KOMBUCHA

½ cup (1 deciliter) lime juice, freshly
  squeezed
¼–½ cup (½–1 deciliter) honey-hibiscus
  syrup, see recipe below
1¼ cups (3 deciliters) kombucha,
  purchased or homemade
2 teaspoons fresh cilantro, finely chopped
1 lime, in wedges
ice cubes
dried hibiscus, sea salt, and coconut sugar
  for the rim of the glass

HONEY-HIBISCUS SYRUP
½ cup (1 deciliter) water
½ cup (1 deciliter) honey
4 tablespoons dried hibiscus
1 teaspoon vanilla powder
1 orange, sliced
¾–1¼ inches (2–3 centimeters) fresh
  ginger, sliced

Start by preparing the syrup. Heat the honey, water, vanilla powder, orange slices, ginger, and dried hibiscus in a small saucepan over medium heat. Let the honey dissolve in the water. Then take the syrup off the heat and let it sit and steep for about 15 minutes. Then strain the syrup through a fine-mesh sieve.

Grind a few dried hibiscus leaves and mix them with equal parts salt and sugar. Rub a lime wedge around the rim of the glass so it's moistened with the lime juice. Then dip the rim of the glass in the salt-sugar-hibiscus mixture.

Put the lime juice, kombucha, cilantro, and honey-hibiscus syrup in a shaker and shake well. Sweeten with more syrup, if needed. Fill the two glasses with ice cubes and pour the drink over.

PEACH-THYME SHRUB

1 pound (450 grams) peaches,
  diced
10 sprigs fresh thyme
1 vanilla pod and the seeds from
  it
1¼–1½ (3–4 centimeters) fresh
  ginger, sliced
½ fresh chili, petite diced
½ cup (1 deciliter) honey, melted
½ cup (1 deciliter) apple cider
  vinegar
sparkling water, fresh peaches,
  crushed ice, and a sprig of
  thyme, optional, for serving

Fill a large, clean jar with the diced peaches, fresh thyme, vanilla beans and pod, ginger, and chili. Pour the melted honey over the fruit and mash it well. If the honey is very thick, melt it in a water bath, beforehand. Let the fruit macerate for about three days in refrigerator. Add the apple cider vinegar on the second day. Shake the glass daily.

After the fruit has macerated well, strain the mixture through a sieve. Optionally add more apple cider vinegar to taste and mood. The flavor will diminish slightly over time.

Pour a few spoonsful of the syrup into a glass, and top with sparkling water, fresh peaches, crushed ice, and a sprig of thyme, if desired.

BLACKBERRY ADAPTOGEN SMOOTHIE

A smoothie a day keeps the doctor away. For breakfast, on the go, between meals, or as ice cream. Imagine that a batch of blended vegetables, fruit, and magical plants can be transformed into a flavor bomb like no other. It feels like a sinful love affair that will never end. The color, the texture, and the pleasing satisfaction of both mind and heart can make me swoon. Exactly why I always look forward to waking up to a new day.

INGREDIENTS
¾ cup (2 deciliters) blackberries, frozen
1 avocado
1–2 lime wedges
4 slices fresh ginger
2 scoops vanilla protein powder
2 tablespoons sea buckthorn, fresh or frozen
2 large handfuls cauliflower, frozen
2 scoops collagen powder
¾ cup (2 deciliters) almond or cashew milk
2 teaspoons lucuma powder
water to desired consistency

Put all of the ingredients in a blender and blend into a velvety smoothie. Divide among two glasses and top with fresh berries, edible flowers, and granola, if desired. Or enjoy it just as it is with no frills.

LOVINGLY SPICED CACAO

Create a peaceful haven amid the hustle and bustle of everyday life and sit down with a cup of liquid magic. This cup of cacao will most likely give you a somewhat different sensory experience than the cups of cocoa you've drunk before. If you choose a good-quality cacao, you may experience how the cacao sharpens your senses and supports your connection to yourself, so you have the opportunity to get in touch with deeper emotional layers. For some, it seems redemptive—for others, uplifting. Allow yourself to be fully present in the now, follow your impulses, and be curious about what appears.

FOR 1 CUP

INGREDIENTS
3 tablespoons–¼ cup (25–35 grams) unprocessed raw cacao beans of good quality
¾ cup (2 deciliters) almond or cashew milk
1 pinch ground cardamom
1 teaspoon ground Ceylon cinnamon
1 teaspoon lucuma powder
1½ teaspoons reishi powder
1 pinch vanilla powder
1 teaspoon coconut oil
1 pinch ground chili
1 pinch ground ginger
1 pinch freshly ground Himalayan salt
coconut sugar

TOPPING
bee pollen or rose petals

Chop the raw cacao into small pieces. Heat the milk up in a saucepan over medium heat and melt the cacao together with the spices and coconut oil. Turn the heat down a bit and stir until the cacao has melted. Be careful not to heat the cacao up too much. This way, the nutrients are preserved as best as possible. Sweeten the cacao with coconut sugar, as desired. Top with bee pollen or rose petals.

MAGICAL
MOON MILK

Get your thoughts together and relax after a long day with warm moon milk so you might have sweet dreams.

WHAT IS MOON MILK?

Moon milk is based on old Ayurvedic principles that a glass of warm milk taken before bedtime—that is, when the moon is up—could help with insomnia and provide a more restful sleep. The main base for the milk drink is milk and honey, but in the modern interpretation, moon milk consists of several basic components where you can experiment with and put your favorite blends together from:

PLANT MILK

Provides a creamy base. I have the best experience with almond milk, oat milk, cashew milk, and coconut milk. If your drink is still a little too thin, you can add collagen powder and/or coconut oil.

CALMING HERBS AND WARM SPICES

Even though many herbs and spices have calming properties, not necessarily all of them have flavors that work well in a creamy dream drink. I have good experience with adaptogenic herbs like reishi and chaga; regular herbs like chamomile, linden flower, lavender, butterfly pea, and rose petals; along with spices like turmeric, cinnamon, nutmeg, ginger, and cardamom.

HEALTHY FATS

Ghee or coconut oil is good for balancing the herbs.

THE SWEETS

If you need to sweeten your drink further, honey, coconut nectar, or syrup can be added.

BASIC METHOD

1. Heat plant milk, herbs, and spices in a small saucepan.
2. Let the drink simmer on low heat for 5 minutes, then remove the pan from the burner. Place a lid over the saucepan and let the drink infuse for 5 to 10 minutes.
3. Strain the drink through a fine-mesh sieve and pour into a cup. Sweeten the drink, if desired, and add coconut oil and/or collagen powder if you want it extra creamy.

MIDNIGHT BLUE MOON MILK

FOR 1 GLASS

1¼ cups (3 deciliters) plant milk
1 teaspoon blue spirulina
1 teaspoon dried chamomile flower
1 teaspoon dried linden flower
1 teaspoon dried lavender
½ teaspoon reishi powder
1 tablespoon collagen powder
  (optional)
1 tablespoon honey (optional)
rose petals for garnish

GOOD NIGHT MOON MILK

FOR 1 GLASS

1¼ cups (3 deciliters) plant milk
½ teaspoon reishi powder
1 teaspoon dried chamomile flower
½ teaspoon vanilla powder or extract
1 tablespoon honey (optional)
1 tablespoon collagen powder (optional)
dried flowers for garnish

CHAI MOON MILK

FOR 1 GLASS

1¼ cups (3 deciliters) plant milk
½ teaspoon ground ginger
½ teaspoon ground Ceylon cinnamon
½ teaspoon reishi powder
dash ground cardamom
dash allspice
dash ground nutmeg
dash ground clove
dash freshly ground pepper
1 teaspoon dried chamomile flower
½ teaspoon vanilla powder or extract
1 tablespoon honey (optional)
1 tablespoon collagen powder (optional)
star anise or cinnamon stick for garnish

REFRESHING ICED TEA

When the sun casts its warm rays over the land, there's a need for extra reinforcement in the form of mouthwatering refreshments. Cool yourself down in the summer heat with this sweet, thirst-quenching iced tea.

YIELDS ABOUT 34 OUNCES, 4¼ CUPS (1 LITER)

INGREDIENTS

2 cups (5 deciliters) freshly brewed herbal tea (for example, cool mint)

3 tablespoons honey

4 sprigs fresh mint or lemon balm

1–2 cups (2½–5 deciliters) cold water

1 blood orange, freshly squeezed

1 lemon, divided (½ freshly squeezed and ½ sliced)

1 vanilla bean, split and scraped

2 cinnamon sticks

Brew the herbal tea you have on hand and let it steep for half an hour, so it becomes robust in flavor. Pour it into a 51-ounce (1½-liter) jar or bottle with a lid. Add the honey and fresh mint or lemon balm and let the herbal tea steep for another half hour before adding the water, blood orange juice, lemon juice and slices, vanilla bean, and cinnamon stick. Put the lid on and let the herbal tea cool down for 1 to 2 hours in the fridge. If necessary, strain the iced tea through a fine-mesh sieve before serving it over ice cubes.

COLD MATCHA-MINT LATTE

I am one of those people who never really learned to love the bitter, brown, and beloved coffee bean. On the other hand, I am quite fond of matcha tea, which is packed with antioxidants. Here, it comes in a cool and refreshing edition, which I almost dare to categorize as the healthiest latte on the market.

ABOUT 2 SMALL OR 1 LARGE GLASSES

MATCHA LATTE
3 teaspoons high-quality
  matcha powder
2 tablespoons hot water
1 teaspoon full-fat coconut milk
1 large tightly packed handful of
  fresh mint leaves
3 tablespoons pistachios
1 teaspoon ginseng powder
2–3 tablespoons honey
ice cubes

TOPPING
fresh mint leaves

Whisk the matcha powder with the 2 tablespoons of hot water, maximum 176°F (80°C) in a small bowl with a bamboo whisk until the powder is dissolved. Set the bowl aside and let the matcha cool slightly. Blend the coconut milk, ginseng, pistachios, and mint leaves so the nuts are ground well. Add the cooled matcha, ice cubes, and honey, and blend again until the ice cubes are crushed.

Top with fresh mint leaves and ice cubes before serving.

FERMENTED BEET KVASS

Earthy, acidic, slightly sweet, and a bit salty. This is probably the best way to describe the flavor of this dark red probiotic drink that is different, fun to make, and makes the stomach happy.

INGREDIENTS

2 large beets (about 1¾–2 cups or 4–5 deciliters), rinsed and diced

1 tablespoon freshly ground Himalayan salt to top

3¼ cups (8 deciliters) filtered or boiled and cooled water

1 fresh ginger root (about ¼ cup or ½ deciliter), sliced

Bring the water to a boil, then let it cool down. Rinse the beets lightly, but do not scrub them. The probiotic bacteria live on the beet skin, so we want to keep the skin on, but be sure there is no soil left on the beets that could negatively affect the fermentation process. Dice the beets and slice the ginger and put them in a sterile canning jar along with the Himalayan salt. Top the jar with water but be sure to leave 1¼ to 1½ inches (3 to 4 centimeters) of space at the top. Close the lid and let the drink ferment for 3 to 5 days on the kitchen counter at room temperature in a dim place. Open the jar every day to release the carbon dioxide produced by the fermentation process and taste the kvass. If it's a bit sweet and slightly acidic, it's certainly ready. White foam can also form on top of the drink, which is completely harmless. Simply remove it with a clean wooden spoon.

Store the drink in the refrigerator for a week, where it will thicken slightly and increase in flavor. Strain the kvass through a fine-mesh sieve and pour into a bottle. You can reuse the diced beets for another batch of kvass or use them in a salad.

Kvass is an old health drink with origins in Eastern Europe. It is often made from bread but is now also found in other versions with fruit, berries, and as in this recipe, with beets.

It's super easy to make kvass, and there are several ways to do it. Some peel the beets, others don't. Some let the fermentation happen under a cloth, others close the canning jar. Some add extra flavor in the form of orange (zest), cinnamon sticks, and spices; others keep it quite simple. I have only tried the method used in this recipe, but feel free to play with method and flavor.

TEPACHE DE PIÑA

You may know about kombucha, but have you heard of tepache de piña? A refreshing, softly bubbling, and sweet-and-sour fermented drink with flavors of pineapple, sweet cinnamon, and star anise. A drink you can enjoy with a good conscience and that makes your everyday a little more festive.

Tepache is a popular Mexican fermented pineapple drink (also called pineapple beer) that is often sold on the street in a plastic bag with a straw in it. It is originally made with the rind of a pineapple and sweetened with cane sugar or brown sugar, which then sits and ferments for a few days. The result is a mildly alcoholic, lightly bubbling drink that resembles a mixture of kombucha, soda water, and beer.

Like other fermented drinks, tepache de piña is packed with healthy probiotic bacteria that help support gut flora and a healthy digestive system.

My basic recipe is on the next page, but I encourage you to play around with other ingredients to see how it develops. It could be cloves, cardamom seeds, or chili, to make the drink extra spicy; apple, mango, or orange (with zest), for extra flavor; or maybe coconut water instead of plain water.

Remember to save about ½–¾ cup (1–2 deciliters) that can act as a "starter" for the next batch, so the fermentation happens faster.

INGREDIENTS

½ cup (1 deciliter) unrefined
   cane sugar or coconut sugar
2¾ cups (6½ deciliters) water
1 large pineapple
1 cinnamon stick
1 tablespoon star anise

Boil 2 cups (5 deciliters) of water along with the unrefined cane sugar in a saucepan and stir until the sugar granules are dissolved. Take the saucepan off the burner, and while the sugar water cools down, cut off the top and bottom of the pineapple. Cut off the rind and eat the fruit as is or save it for another recipe. Only the rind is used in this recipe. Add it to a large, sanitized canning jar with the pineapple rinds, along with the cinnamon stick and star anise. Pour the sugar water over, along with another ⅔ cup (1½ deciliters) of boiled, cooled water. Cover the opening of the jar with a cloth and a rubber band and let the drink ferment for 2 to 3 days on the kitchen counter at room temperature, or until the drink starts to bubble and forms foam on the surface. Check it regularly, since the fermentation depends on many factors, like temperature and the ripeness of the fruit, et cetera. If you let it ferment for a week or longer, the drink will become more alcoholic, and if it stands for a month or longer, it will develop into a delicious pineapple vinegar.

Remove the foam from the surface with a clean wooden spoon before straining the drink through a fine-meshed sieve and pouring into bottles. Store the drink in the refrigerator and serve it with ice cubes and freshly squeezed lemon or make a delicious cocktail with tequila or rum.

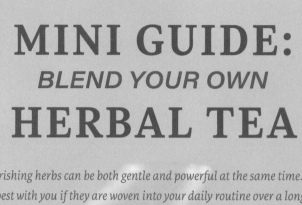

MINI GUIDE:
BLEND YOUR OWN
HERBAL TEA

Nourishing herbs can be both gentle and powerful at the same time. They work best with you if they are woven into your daily routine over a long period of time, where they can be allowed to strengthen your body with vitamins, minerals, and essential nutrients that can have a positive influence on your physical and mental health. Working with herbs offers no guarantee and is not a quick fix, but an invitation to lift your well-being and your self-care, if you dare to be a little curious about the herbs, and not least, yourself.

It can feel a little bit magical and almost meditative to blend your own herbal tea. An entirely unique blend for you, whether you need to create more peace of mind, fill your body's cells with energy, or strengthen your focus. But why should you actually blend your own tea?

Even though it's easy and convenient to buy ready-made tea bags in the supermarket, the non-organic kind can, unfortunately, be full of pesticides and additives that are artificially produced. When you blend your own tea, you ensure that the herbs are of high quality, taste fresher, and have a better nutritional profile. You can buy most herbs in bulk at the health food store or online, so you don't need to have your own herb garden and your own drying room at home to get started.

If you've never tried blending your own tea before, my recommendation is always to start out simply with 2 to 3 herbs, until you get to know them and feel how your body interacts with them.

Measure in parts so you can always scale up or down, depending on whether you want to make a cup or a little jar of a blend. The herbs should also be roughly the same size in your blend, so you may need to grind the larger ones in a mortar and pestle. You can use both fresh and dried herbs for your freshly brewed tea. Store your herbal blend in an airtight jar in a dark place.

STEP 1
The very first step to putting together your own herbal tea is choosing an herb to serve as a base. This herb should be the most active ingredient in the blend. Choose about 3 parts of your chosen base herb.

STEP 2
Then, choose a few synergistic and supporting herbs that work well with your herbal base and what you think might taste good together. Select 1 to 2 parts of the supporting herbs.

STEP 3
Finally, select an herb that adds flavor. It can also be dried fruit pieces or zest to sweeten the tea. Choose ¼ to 1 part of the flavoring herbs.

STEP 4
Blend about 1 teaspoon or 1 tablespoon of tea with 1 to 1¼ cups (2½ to 3 deciliters) of water. Let the tea steep for at least 15 minutes in order to provide therapeutic benefits. It can also steep for up to 1 hour if you want a more robust flavor.

HERBS FOR VARIOUS NEEDS

There are an infinite number of herbs out there. Here's a selection of some of the ones I've tried out. Remember that we each have different needs, so this guide is purely for exploring what feels nice and just right for you. Always consult a professional health advisor if you are in doubt about which herbs are best for your individual needs.

DIGESTION
Chamomile

Fennel

Ginger

Licorice

Peppermint/mint

SLEEP
Lavender

Passionflower

Rosebuds

Valerian root

FOCUS
Basil

Ginkgo biloba

Gotu kola

Rosemary

IMMUNE DEFENSE
Astragalus

Echinacea

Elderflower/elderberry

Ginger

ANXIETY AND UNREST
Chamomile

Lavender

Lemon balm/heart's delight

Oat straw

CLEANSING
Burdock root

Dandelion/dandelion root

Stinging nettle

Yarrow

INFLAMMATION
Cinnamon

Clove

Hibiscus

Turmeric

Go-To Recipes

DIGESTIVE TEA

to calm the stomach and strengthen the memory

1 part dried peppermint
½ part dried fennel
½ part dried cilantro (coriander)
  seeds

CALMING TEA

to quell restlessness and racing thoughts in the body while improving sleep

1 part dried chamomile
½ part dried lavender
½ part dried mint

or

1 part dried chamomile
½ part dried lemon balm
⅓ part dried rosebuds
1 cinnamon stick, finely chopped

FOCUSING TEA

to sharpen the mind and raise the energy

½ cup (1 deciliter) dried peppermint
½ part dried or powdered gotu kola
½ part dried or powdered ginkgo biloba
¼ part dried rosemary

SLEEP-INDUCING TEA

to relax body and mind and unwind after a long day

½ cup (1 deciliter) dried lemon balm
½ part dried passionflower
½ part dried chamomile
¼ part dried mint

CLEANSING TEA

to support the liver's cleansing process

1 part dried dandelion root
¼ part dried burdock root
¼ part dried ginger

HOT APPLE CIDER
with chaga

This recipe does not require much finesse, but a good deal of patience. Then, you just have to wait for your home to be enveloped in a sweet aroma, and you can sip this warm drink. If you have a four-legged friend or a fireplace at home, the coziness barometer will skyrocket.

YIELDS 1 LARGE PITCHER

INGREDIENTS
8–10 apples, quartered
1 orange, quartered
1 tablespoon chaga powder
3 cinnamon sticks
6 cloves
½ teaspoon ground nutmeg
1 teaspoon ground allspice
1 teaspoon reishi powder
3–6 tablespoons maple syrup
  or honey
water to cover

Put all of the ingredients in a saucepan, cover with water, and stir. Allow the apple cider to simmer over medium heat for about 2 to 2½ hours. Take the saucepan off the burner and let the cider infuse for a further ½ to 1 hour before straining the drink through a fine-meshed sieve—possibly twice to make it as clear as possible. Flavor with maple syrup or honey if the apple cider needs to be sweetened further. Store it in the fridge for up to a week. Enjoy it hot or cold.

Reference List

Books

Ballegaard, A.: *Urtelykke*, 2019, Aronsen.

Benzie, I. & Wachtel-Galor, S.: *Herbal Medicine*, 2011, CRC Press.

Bergmark, M.: *Læge-urter og urte-te*, 1965, Rosenkilde og Bagger.

Cech, R.: *Making Plant Medicine*, 2000, Horizon Herbs.

Chevallier, A.: *Politikens bog om lægeplanter*, 1998, Politikens Forlag.

Gladstar, R.: *Medicinal Herbs: A Beginner's Guide*, 2012, Storey Publishing Llc.

Gladstar, R. & Hirsch, P.: *Planting the Future: Saving Our Medicinal Herbs*, 2000, Healing Arts Press.

Green, J.: *The Herbal Medicine-Maker's Handbook*, 2000, Crossing Press.

Hartung, T.: *Growing 101 Herbs that Heal*, 2000, Storey Publishing.

Hoffmann, D.: *Holistic Herbal: A Safe and Practical Guide to Making and Using Herbal Remedies*, 2003, HarperCollins Publishers.

Hoffmann, D.: *Medical Herbalism: The Science and Practice of Herbal Medicine*, 2003 Healing Arts Press.

McIntyre, A.: *Mere energi med urter*, 2006, Gyldendal.

Olesen, A.: *Krydderurter*, 2010, Politiken.

Pedersen, Carl Th.: *Krydderier fra A til Z*, 2021, Turbine.

Pugliese, S.: *Krydderurter*, 2016, Muusmann.

Swahn, J. Ö.: A*lverdens krydderier*, 1999, Sesam.

Tvedegaard, L.: *Krydderurter*, 2013, Koustrup & Co.

Verinder, E.: *Plants for the People*, 2020, Thames & Hudson.

Winston, D.: *Adaptogens*, 2019, Healing Arts Press.

Wood, M.: *The Book of Herbal Wisdom*, 1997, North Atlantic Books.

Internet resources

The Herbal Academy: www.theherbalacademy.com

U.S. National Library of Medicine: www.nim.nih.gov

Urtegartneriet: www.urtegartneriet.dk

Scientific articles

Beaty, D. & Foutch, S.: The Benefits of Soaking Nuts and Seeds, 2013.

Gupta, R.K., Gangoliya, S.S., Singh, N.K.: Reduction of phytic acid and enhancement of bioavailable micronutrients in food grains, 2013.

A special big thank-you

My stubborn, tenacious, and absolutely fantastic editor, **Rikke Luna Hall Mortensen**, who from day one believed in me and the concept of the book. This book is allowed to unfold because of you.

Photographer **Rikke Westesen**. The warmest, happiest, and most creative being I have met in a long time. With her tireless energy and fondness for crooked and crumpled ceramics, she has captured in the pictures precisely the atmosphere I dreamed of for the book.

Karin Hald, who has waved her graphic magic wand and set up the book with a playful yet nevertheless simple expression.

The entire team at **Turbine** for believing that there is room for yet another green cookbook on the market.

My wonderful friend, **Cecilia**, who, with curiosity and an eye for detail, stepped in at the last minute to help me with cooking.

KoRo, which, among other things has generously sponsored superfoods, nuts, and plant butter for the book's recipes. **NatureSource**, which has contributed a large part of the basic products used in the recipes. Everything from various liquid delights, like vinegar, coconut cream, and kombucha, to snacks like crispy crackers, luscious jackfruit, and colorful noodles. **Fresh.Land**, which has enriched the recipes with all kinds of fresh fruit and vegetables, and which made the flavor experience all the better. **Maison Loüno**, which has brought healthy and flavorful rituals for self-care into my everyday life with its unique matcha and cacao blends and adaptogenic herbs.

The biggest thanks must go to my husband, **Rasmus**, and my mother, **Bettina**. Thank you for exposing your taste buds to countless test tastings, for cheering me on when I occasionally felt so far from the finish line that I just had to destroy a couple of already deformed pot holders or didn't feel like cooking for several weeks, for your invaluable and persistent efforts on some intense photo days, and not least for your endless love.

Without you, no cookbook.

Recipe list